VALUE YOUR TIME

It's Limited

Cregg Hampton

DEDICATION

To all those who have come to understand the true value of time, this book is dedicated to you.

To the dreamers, the doers, and the seekers of purpose, may these pages inspire you to make the most of each fleeting moment.

To those who have embarked on the journey of self-discovery, personal growth, and continuous improvement, may this book serve as a guiding light along the path.

To the busy parents, the ambitious professionals, and the relentless entrepreneurs, may you find solace in the wisdom shared here and discover the art of harmonizing work and personal life.

To the students and young learners, may you embrace the lessons of time management early on and forge a path to a successful and fulfilling future.

To the mentors, teachers, and coaches, who tirelessly impart their knowledge and wisdom, may this book be a tool to empower others with the gift of effective time management.

To the advocates of well-being and mental health, may the principles of valuing time contribute to a world where balance and self-care are cherished above all.

To the believers in the potential of each human soul, may this book inspire you to recognize that time is a canvas upon which dreams are woven and destinies are crafted.

To my family and friends, whose unwavering support has been a constant source of strength and inspiration, thank you for sharing in this journey.

And finally, to the readers, without whom this book would remain silent and unexplored, may you find the courage to embrace the time you have been given, cherish each passing moment, and value the timeless gift of time itself.

With heartfelt gratitude,

CREGG HAMPTON

EPIGRAPH PAGE

"We must use time wisely and forever realize that the time is always ripe to do right."
Nelson Mandela

"Time is what we want most, but what we use worst."
William Penn

"Your time is limited; don't waste it living someone else's life."
Steve Jobs

"Lost time is never found again."
Benjamin Franklin

"Time is the most valuable thing a man can spend."
Theophrastus

"Time management is life management."
Robin Sharma

"Time is the scarcest resource and unless it is managed, nothing else can be managed."
Peter Drucker

"Time is what keeps everything from happening at once."
Ray Cummings

"The key is not in spending time, but in investing it."
Stephen R. Covey

"Time is the wisest counselor of all."
Pericles

"Time flies over us, but leaves its shadow behind."
Nathaniel Hawthorne

"The trouble is, you think you have time."
Buddha

"Time is a created thing. To say 'I don't have time,' is like saying, 'I don't want to.'"
Lao Tzu

"Time is the school in which we learn, time is the fire in which we burn."
Delmore Schwartz

"Time is a currency you can only spend once. Make sure you invest it, rather than merely spending it."
Craig D. Lounsbrough

"Time is the longest distance between two places."
Tennessee Williams

"Time is more valuable than money. You can get more money, but you cannot get more time."
Jim Rohn

Contents

Preface

Time is an elusive concept - intangible yet omnipresent, fleeting yet ever-present. It is the one constant in our lives, yet it slips through our fingers like sand. In a world where the pace of life seems to quicken with each passing day, it has become increasingly essential to pause, reflect, and appreciate the true value of time.

This book, "Value Your Time," is born out of a deep conviction that time is our most precious resource and that how we choose to use it shapes the trajectory of our lives. As the author, I have been on a personal quest to understand the significance of time management and its impact on our well-being, productivity, and overall happiness. Through my own experiences and observations, I have come to recognize the transformative power of valuing our time.

In the pages that follow, we will embark on a journey of exploration, self-discovery, and growth. We will delve into the various facets of time management, examining the principles, strategies, and mindset needed to make the most of our limited time. This book is not a one-size-fits-all solution, but rather a collection of insights, tools, and perspectives to help you navigate the complexities of time and to enable you to forge your path towards a more fulfilling life.

The Nature of Time

We begin by contemplating the elusive nature of time and how our perception of it shapes our reality. By understanding that time is a finite resource, we can begin to appreciate its true value and become more intentional in how we spend it.

Understanding Time

In Chapter 2, we delve into the mechanics of time and explore how it is measured and perceived across cultures and history. By gaining a deeper understanding of time's intricacies, we can cultivate a more mindful relationship with it.

The Value of Time

In Chapter 3, we explore the inherent value of time and how it influences our decision-making and priorities. We examine the opportunity cost of our choices and learn to cherish the moments that truly matter.

Setting Priorities

Chapter 4 focuses on the art of setting priorities and making conscious choices that align with our values and aspirations. By understanding the power of focus and discernment, we can direct our time and energy towards what truly matters.

Goal Setting

In Chapter 5, we explore the role of goal setting in guiding our actions and shaping our future. We learn how to create clear and actionable goals that inspire us to pursue our dreams with purpose and determination.

Time Audit

In Chapter 6, we conduct a time audit to assess how we currently allocate our time and identify opportunities for improvement. By analyzing our time usage, we can make informed decisions on how to optimize our routines and habits.

Overcoming Procrastination

Procrastination is a common roadblock to effective time management, and in Chapter 7, we confront the underlying causes of procrastination and learn strategies to overcome it. By developing self-awareness and cultivating discipline, we can break free from the cycle of delay and seize the moment.

Avoiding Time Wasters

In Chapter 8, we identify common time wasters and learn how to minimize distractions and unproductive activities. By eliminating time-wasting habits, we can free up valuable time for more meaningful pursuits.

Effective Planning Techniques

Chapter 9 introduces a variety of planning techniques, including time blocking, to help us structure our days and weeks efficiently. By organizing our time thoughtfully, we can strike a balance between productivity and rest.

Delegation and Outsourcing

Recognizing that we cannot do it all, Chapter 10 explores the power of delegation and outsourcing. By entrusting tasks to others, we can focus on our strengths and leverage the expertise of those around us.

Saying No

In Chapter 11, we explore the art of saying no and setting boundaries to protect our time and energy. By asserting our priorities, we can avoid overcommitment and create space for what truly matters.

Time Blocking Techniques

Chapter 12 delves deeper into time blocking, a powerful method for structuring our days and optimizing productivity. By allocating dedicated time to specific tasks, we can harness the full potential of focused work.

Managing Distractions

In Chapter 13, we confront the pervasive issue of distractions in our digital age. By adopting strategies to minimize interruptions, we can safeguard our focus and maintain productivity.

Efficient Communication

Chapter 14 emphasizes the importance of effective communication in time management. By practicing assertiveness and clarity, we can streamline our interactions and avoid misunderstandings.

Healthy Work-Life Balance

In Chapter 15, we explore the concept of work-life integration, seeking harmony rather than division between our personal and professional lives. By nurturing all aspects of our well-being, we can create a more fulfilling and sustainable lifestyle.

Mindfulness and Time Awareness

Chapter 16 highlights the role of mindfulness in enhancing our time awareness and presence. By embracing the here and now, we can cultivate a deeper appreciation for the moments that shape our lives.

Maximizing Productivity

In Chapter 17, we uncover strategies to maximize productivity without sacrificing well-being. By optimizing our workflows and routines, we can achieve more with less effort.

The Power of Habits

Chapter 18 explores the profound impact of habits on our time management practices. By cultivating positive habits and breaking free from negative ones, we can create a solid foundation for success.

Managing Stress and Burnout

In Chapter 19, we address the importance of managing stress and avoiding burnout. By nurturing resilience and self-care, we can maintain a healthy relationship with time and sustain our well-being.

Learning to Relax

Chapter 20 emphasizes the significance of relaxation and leisure in a well-balanced life. By carving out time for rejuvenation, we can find harmony amidst life's demands.

Flexibility and Adaptability

In Chapter 21, we embrace the virtues of flexibility and adaptability in our time management journey. By accepting life's unpredictability, we can adjust our plans and approach with grace.

The Impact of Technology

Chapter 22 examines the influence of technology on our relationship with time. By harnessing technology mindfully, we can use it as a tool for productivity rather than a source of distraction.

Continuous Improvement

In Chapter 23, we adopt a growth mindset and commit to continuous improvement in our time management practices. By learning from experiences and seeking new insights, we can continuously refine our approach.

Teaching Time Management Skills

Chapter 24 explores the significance of teaching time management skills to others. By sharing our knowledge and empowering others, we can contribute to a more mindful and productive society.

Conclusion

As we reach the end of our journey, the Conclusion chapter reinforces the core messages of this book and encourages us to embrace a time-valuing lifestyle.

In writing "Value Your Time," my ultimate aspiration is for readers to embark on their journey of self-discovery, armed with the tools and insights needed to make the most of their limited time. Whether you are a student seeking to excel in academics, a professional striving for work-life harmony, an entrepreneur navigating the challenges of business, or an individual seeking fulfillment and happiness, the principles of valuing time can empower you to unlock your fullest potential.

I invite you to approach this book with an open mind and a willingness to reflect on your relationship with time. As you embark on this transformative journey, I hope that "Value Your Time" will serve as a guiding light, illuminating the path towards a more meaningful, purposeful, and fulfilling life.

Remember, time is a precious gift, and it is up to each of us to use it wisely and cherish every moment.

CREGG HAMPTON

∞ ∞ ∞

Introduction

Tick-tock, tick-tock—the constant rhythm of time is the heartbeat of our existence. From the moment we take our first breath to the last, time accompanies us on our journey through life. Yet, despite its ubiquitous presence, we often find ourselves struggling to harness its power, desperately seeking more of it while feeling like it slips through our fingers like sand. Time is limited, and once it's gone, it can never be reclaimed. This fundamental truth serves as the foundation of our exploration in this book—"Value Your Time."

In a world that seems to move at an ever-increasing pace, we are bombarded with demands, distractions, and commitments that leave us feeling overwhelmed, stressed, and unsure of how to manage our time effectively. The pressures of modern life make it easy to fall into a cycle of busyness, where we constantly chase the illusion of productivity without truly considering the value of the moments we spend.

"Value Your Time" is a comprehensive guide that delves into the art and science of time management, offering practical strategies and profound insights to help you appreciate and utilize your time more intentionally. As the author, I have spent years exploring the intricacies of time and its impact on our lives. Through personal experiences, research, and observations, I have come to recognize that time management is not merely about squeezing more tasks into our days—it is about aligning our actions with our values, dreams, and aspirations.

The Nature of Time

We begin our journey by contemplating the enigmatic nature of time. Time is both a relentless force and a precious gift, and by understanding its essence, we can develop a more profound appreciation for the moments that shape our lives.

Understanding Time

In Chapter 2, we embark on an exploration of the concept of time itself. We delve into the intricacies of time's measurement, its perception across cultures and civilizations, and how it serves as the thread that weaves the tapestry of human history.

The Value of Time

Chapter 3 delves into the inherent value of time and how it influences our decisions, priorities, and sense of purpose. By recognizing the opportunity cost of our choices, we can elevate our time management practices and cherish the moments that truly matter.

Setting Priorities

In Chapter 4, we delve into the art of setting priorities. Time management is about more than just efficiency; it is about identifying what truly matters in our lives and aligning our actions accordingly. By discovering the power of focus and discernment, we can direct our time and energy towards what genuinely brings us fulfillment.

Goal Setting

Chapter 5 takes us on a journey of goal setting—a process that empowers us to envision our desired future and create a roadmap to get there. By setting clear and inspiring goals, we can ignite the flames of purpose and motivation that drive us towards success.

Time Audit

Chapter 6 introduces the powerful concept of a time audit, a process that allows us to take a close look at how we currently spend our time. By conducting this introspective examination, we can identify inefficiencies, time-wasting activities, and opportunities for improvement.

Overcoming Procrastination

Procrastination is the nemesis of effective time management. In Chapter 7, we confront the underlying causes of procrastination and learn strategies to overcome this insidious habit. By fostering self-awareness and cultivating discipline, we can break free from the grip of procrastination and embrace the power of the present moment.

Avoiding Time Wasters

Chapter 8 is dedicated to identifying and avoiding time wasters —those distractions and unproductive activities that chip away at our precious time. By eliminating time-wasting habits, we can reclaim valuable moments for pursuits that truly bring us joy and fulfillment.

Effective Planning Techniques

Chapter 9 introduces a range of effective planning techniques, including time blocking and other productivity tools. By thoughtfully organizing our time and routines, we can strike a balance between productivity and well-being, optimizing our performance without sacrificing self-care.

Delegation and Outsourcing

Recognizing that we cannot do it all, Chapter 10 explores the power of delegation and outsourcing. By entrusting tasks to others, we can free up time to focus on our strengths and passions, leading to increased productivity and personal growth.

Saying No

Chapter 11 emphasizes the importance of setting boundaries and embracing the art of saying no. By asserting our priorities and protecting our time, we can avoid overcommitment and create space for the activities that align with our true desires.

Time Blocking Techniques

Chapter 12 delves deeper into time blocking—a powerful technique that allows us to allocate dedicated time to specific tasks and responsibilities. By harnessing the potential of focused work, we can achieve more with greater efficiency and effectiveness.

Managing Distractions

Chapter 13 explores the pervasive issue of distractions in our technology-driven world. By adopting strategies to minimize interruptions and cultivate focus, we can safeguard our attention and productivity.

Efficient Communication

In Chapter 14, we emphasize the importance of effective communication in time management. By improving our communication skills, we can streamline interactions, reduce misunderstandings, and enhance collaboration.

Healthy Work-Life Balance

Chapter 15 focuses on cultivating a healthy work-life balance— a state of harmony between personal and professional pursuits. By nurturing all aspects of our well-being, we can lead more fulfilling and sustainable lives.

Mindfulness and Time Awareness

Chapter 16 highlights the role of mindfulness in enhancing our time awareness and presence. By embracing the present moment, we can find greater joy and appreciation in the moments that shape our lives.

Maximizing Productivity

In Chapter 17, we delve into strategies for maximizing productivity without sacrificing well-being. By optimizing our workflows and routines, we can achieve more while maintaining balance and avoiding burnout.

The Power of Habits

Chapter 18 explores the profound impact of habits on our time management practices. By cultivating positive habits and breaking free from negative ones, we can create a strong foundation for success and personal growth.

Managing Stress and Burnout

Chapter 19 addresses the importance of managing stress and avoiding burnout. By fostering resilience and practicing self-care, we can maintain a healthy relationship with time and preserve our well-being.

Learning to Relax

Chapter 20 emphasizes the significance of relaxation and leisure in our fast-paced lives. By carving out time for rejuvenation, we can find balance and replenish our energy to face life's challenges.

Flexibility and Adaptability

In Chapter 21, we embrace the virtues of flexibility and adaptability. By accepting life's unpredictability and adjusting our plans with grace, we can navigate change with resilience and ease.

The Impact of Technology

Chapter 22 examines the impact of technology on our relationship with time. By using technology mindfully, we can leverage its benefits without falling prey to its addictive nature.

Continuous Improvement

Chapter 23 advocates for a growth mindset and a commitment to continuous improvement in our time management practices. By learning from experiences and seeking new insights, we can continually refine our approach and become better stewards of our time.

Teaching Time Management Skills

Chapter 24 explores the significance of teaching time management skills to others. By sharing our knowledge and empowering others, we can contribute to a more mindful and productive society.

Conclusion

As we reach the end of this journey, the Conclusion chapter reaffirms the core messages of "Value Your Time" and serves as a call to action. We reflect on the transformative power of valuing our time and the profound impact it can have on our lives.

This book is an invitation to embark on a transformative journey—one that will lead you towards a more intentional, fulfilling, and purpose-driven life. Whether you are a student seeking academic excellence, a professional striving for work-life harmony, an entrepreneur navigating the challenges of business, or an individual seeking happiness and fulfillment, the principles of time management presented here are universal, adaptable, and empowering.

As you delve into the pages that follow, I encourage you to approach this exploration with an open mind and a willingness to embrace change. The insights, strategies, and wisdom contained within these pages have the potential to transform the way you perceive and use time. By cultivating a deep appreciation for the value of your time and taking intentional steps towards effective time management, you can unlock your full potential and embrace a life of purpose, joy, and fulfillment.

Thank you for joining me on this journey. Let us now embark on the path of valuing our time and creating a life well-lived.

CREGG HAMPTON

∞ ∞ ∞

Prologue

Tick, tock, tick, tock—the rhythmic beat of a clock echoes through the corridors of time, a constant reminder of the precious and finite nature of our existence. Time is the most valuable resource we possess, yet it often slips through our fingers, leaving us with a sense of urgency and a longing to make the most of each moment.

Welcome to "Value Your Time," a transformative journey of self-discovery and empowerment in the realm of time management and personal growth. In these pages, we will embark on a quest to unlock the secrets of time, to understand its true essence, and to harness its power to lead fulfilling and purpose-driven lives.

As the author of this book, I stand before you not as an all-knowing guru, but as a fellow traveler on this journey. My path has been shaped by experiences both triumphs and tribulations that have led me to recognize the immense value of time in our lives. Through countless encounters with individuals seeking guidance in time management, I have witnessed the transformative impact that intentional living can have.

The concept of time has intrigued humanity for millennia, and philosophers, scientists, and thinkers across cultures and ages have pondered its nature. From ancient civilizations to modern-day researchers, the exploration of time has revealed its enigmatic and profound qualities.

In "Value Your Time," we will not merely measure time in minutes and hours, but we will delve into the richness of time as a concept that intertwines with our thoughts, emotions, and actions. We will explore how our perception of time shapes our reality and how our choices influence the trajectory of our lives.

Time, like a flowing river, moves relentlessly onward, never stopping or rewinding. It is a resource that cannot be stored, exchanged, or replenished. We must learn to cherish it, respect it, and utilize it wisely, for once a moment passes, it becomes an indelible part of our history.

But what does it truly mean to value time? To value time is to recognize its inherent worth and the potential it holds. It is to understand that each moment is an opportunity for growth, for connection, for creation, and for impact.

In a world that often emphasizes productivity, busyness, and instant gratification, it is easy to lose sight of the value of time. We find ourselves racing through our days, constantly striving to achieve more, yet often feeling unfulfilled and disconnected from our true selves.

"Value Your Time" is a call to break free from the chains of urgency and to embrace the gift of the present moment. It is an invitation to step back, reflect, and realign our priorities with our values and aspirations. Through intentional time management and personal growth, we can create a life that is truly meaningful and aligned with our deepest desires.

Throughout this book, we will explore a wide range of topics and strategies related to time management. From setting priorities to overcoming procrastination, from managing distractions to embracing mindfulness, each chapter will offer insights and practical tools to optimize your time and enhance your life.

Chapter 1: Understanding Time - We will delve into the nature of time itself, exploring its dimensions, perception, and cultural significance. By understanding time's fluidity and complexity, we can begin to appreciate its value and the role it plays in shaping our lives.

Chapter 2: The Value of Time - In this chapter, we will explore the intrinsic value of time and the cost of squandering it. By recognizing time as a finite and precious resource, we can cultivate a deeper appreciation for each passing moment.

Chapter 3: Setting Priorities - Prioritization is key to effective time management. We will learn how to identify our core values and goals, aligning our actions with what truly matters to us.

Chapter 4: Goal Setting - Goals provide a roadmap for our journey through time. In this chapter, we will explore the art of setting SMART goals and how they can serve as beacons of focus and motivation.

Chapter 5: Time Audit - A time audit helps us gain insight into how we spend our days. By identifying time sinks and patterns, we can make informed decisions to optimize our daily routines.

Chapter 6: Overcoming Procrastination - Procrastination is the thief of time, robbing us of opportunities for growth and achievement. We will explore strategies to overcome this common challenge and take proactive steps towards success.

Chapter 7: Avoiding Time Wasters - From mindless scrolling to excessive meetings, there are countless time-wasting activities that hinder our productivity. In this chapter, we will identify and eliminate these obstacles to regain control of our time.

Chapter 8: Effective Planning Techniques - Planning is the cornerstone of time management. We will explore different planning methods and tools to enhance our efficiency and effectiveness.

Chapter 9: Delegation and Outsourcing - We cannot do everything ourselves. By delegating tasks and outsourcing, we free up valuable time and focus on our unique strengths and passions.

Chapter 10: Saying No - Boundaries are essential in protecting our time and well-being. We will learn the art of saying no gracefully and assertively, ensuring that our time is spent on what truly matters.

Chapter 11: Time Blocking Techniques - Time blocking is a powerful tool to structure our days and focus on specific tasks. We will explore various time blocking methods to maximize our productivity and creativity.

Chapter 12: Managing Distractions - Distractions are omnipresent in our modern world. In this chapter, we will explore strategies to manage and minimize distractions, creating an environment conducive to deep work and focus.

Chapter 13: Efficient Communication - Clear and effective communication saves time and prevents misunderstandings. We will explore communication strategies that enhance productivity and strengthen relationships.

Chapter 14: Healthy Work-Life Balance - A healthy work-life balance is crucial for overall well-being. We will explore strategies to harmonize our personal and professional lives, nurturing both aspects of our existence.

Chapter 15: Mindfulness and Time Awareness - Mindfulness brings us into the present moment, enhancing our awareness of time and its passing. We will explore mindfulness practices to cultivate a deeper connection with each moment.

Chapter 16: Maximizing Productivity - Productivity is not about doing more but doing what matters most. We will explore principles and techniques to maximize our productivity and achieve meaningful results.

Chapter 17: The Power of Habits - Habits shape our daily

routines and influence our lives. We will explore the science of habit formation and how to cultivate positive habits that support our goals.

Chapter 18: Managing Stress and Burnout - Stress can erode our well-being and efficiency. In this chapter, we will explore stress management techniques to build resilience and prevent burnout.

Chapter 19: Learning to Relax - Rest and relaxation are essential for renewal and creativity. We will explore the art of relaxation and how it contributes to our overall productivity and happiness.

Chapter 20: Flexibility and Adaptability - Time is unpredictable, and life throws unexpected challenges our way. We will learn to embrace flexibility and adaptability as essential skills for navigating change.

Chapter 21: The Impact of Technology - Technology has revolutionized how we experience time. In this chapter, we will explore the effects of technology on our lives and how to use it mindfully.

Chapter 22: Continuous Improvement - Growth is a lifelong journey. We will explore the importance of continuous improvement and the pursuit of excellence in all aspects of life.

Chapter 23: Teaching Time Management Skills - Empowering others with time management skills enriches not only their lives but also our own. We will explore ways to share the principles of "Value Your Time" with those around us.

Chapter 24: Conclusion - As we conclude our journey, we will reflect on the transformative power of valuing time and embracing personal growth. We will celebrate the progress we have made and look towards a future of purpose, joy, and fulfillment.

Join me on this exploration of time and its profound impact on our lives. As we turn the pages of "Value Your Time," let us embrace the present moment, mindful of the time that flows within and around us. May we emerge from this journey with a renewed appreciation for the gift of time and the wisdom to embrace each moment with purpose, intention, and joy.

With warmest regards,

CREGG HAMPTON

Foreword

In the ever-accelerating pace of the modern world, time has become one of our most valuable and yet elusive resources. It seems as though there are never enough hours in a day to accomplish everything we desire, and the constant stream of distractions makes it challenging to focus on what truly matters. The need to manage our time effectively has never been more critical, and in "Value Your Time," Cregg Hampton offers a compelling and insightful guide to help us navigate the complexities of time management and reclaim control over our lives.

As I have had the privilege of observing Cregg's journey as both a friend and a mentor, I can attest to his deep passion for the subject of time management and personal development. Through countless conversations and discussions, it became apparent that Cregg's understanding of time transcends the conventional notion of mere productivity. Instead, he views time as a catalyst for personal growth, fulfillment, and the realization of our aspirations.

"Value Your Time" is more than just a practical guide; it is a philosophical exploration of the essence of time and its significance in shaping our lives. Cregg beautifully weaves together personal anecdotes, scientific research, and timeless wisdom to offer readers a comprehensive and holistic perspective on time management. Each chapter is a treasure trove of insights, strategies, and practical exercises that empower readers to embrace the value of time and make intentional choices that align with their goals and values.

In this book, Cregg urges us to step away from the relentless pursuit of productivity for productivity's sake and encourages us to embark on a journey of self-discovery. By understanding the essence of time and our relationship with it, we can cultivate a deep appreciation for the present moment and become more intentional in our actions. Through his writing, Cregg challenges us to evaluate our priorities, confront our fears and limitations, and embrace a mindset of growth and continuous improvement.

One of the most remarkable aspects of "Value Your Time" is its inclusivity—it speaks to individuals from all walks of life. Whether you are a student striving for academic excellence, a professional seeking work-life balance, an entrepreneur juggling multiple responsibilities, or someone simply searching for a more fulfilling existence, the wisdom contained within this book is both relevant and transformative.

The journey through "Value Your Time" is not a solitary one. Cregg invites readers to reflect on their experiences, engage in thought-provoking exercises, and develop actionable plans for optimizing their time management. As a reader, you will find yourself immersed in a dialogue with the author, discovering new insights and perspectives that will resonate deeply with your own journey.

As you embark on this journey with "Value Your Time," I encourage you to approach the book with an open mind and a willingness to challenge your assumptions about time and productivity. Embrace the principles presented here with curiosity and a sense of adventure, knowing that every step you take towards valuing your time will lead you closer to a life of purpose, fulfillment, and balance.

In closing, I extend my deepest gratitude to Cregg Hampton for sharing his wisdom, passion, and expertise through "Value Your Time." This book has the power to transform the way we view time and its impact on our lives, and I am confident that its message will resonate with readers around the world. May this book be a guiding light on your journey towards embracing the value of time and living a life of intention and meaning.

With warmest regards,

SAM GARDNER

Author of "Success Habits"

Value Your Time

IT'S LIMITED

Cragg Hampton

IT'S LIMITED

VALUE YOUR TIME

CREGG HAMPTON

CREGG HAMPTON

BOOK OVERVIEW

CHAPTER 1: INTRODUCTION

In this chapter, we will explore the concept of time as a limited resource and discuss the importance of valuing and managing our time effectively. We will outline the objectives of the book and provide an overview of the subsequent chapters.

CHAPTER 2: UNDERSTANDING TIME

Here, we delve into the nature of time and its perception. We explore various philosophical and scientific theories about time and how our perception of it affects our actions and decisions.

CHAPTER 3: THE VALUE OF TIME

In this chapter, we discuss the inherent value of time and why it is crucial to recognize and appreciate its worth. We examine the concept of opportunity cost and how every decision we make involves a trade-off of our limited time.

CHAPTER 4: SETTING PRIORITIES

Effective time management begins with setting priorities. We discuss strategies for identifying and prioritizing tasks based on their importance and urgency. We also explore the Eisenhower Matrix and other frameworks for prioritization.

CHAPTER 5: GOAL SETTING

Goals provide us with a sense of direction and purpose. In this chapter, we delve into the process of goal setting and how it can help us allocate our time and efforts towards meaningful objectives. We provide practical tips for setting SMART goals.

CHAPTER 6: TIME AUDIT

To effectively manage our time, we must first understand how we currently spend it. We discuss the concept of a time audit and provide tools and techniques for analyzing and evaluating our daily activities to identify areas for improvement.

CHAPTER 7: OVERCOMING PROCRASTINATION

Procrastination can be a significant obstacle to valuing our time. In this chapter, we explore the root causes of procrastination and provide strategies and techniques for overcoming it. We also discuss the importance of discipline and self-motivation.

CHAPTER 8: AVOIDING TIME WASTERS

In today's digital age, there are numerous distractions that can consume our time unnecessarily. We discuss common time wasters such as social media, excessive multitasking, and unproductive meetings. We provide practical tips for minimizing these distractions and reclaiming our time.

CHAPTER 9: EFFECTIVE PLANNING TECHNIQUES

Effective planning is the key to optimizing our use of time. In this chapter, we explore various planning techniques, including to-do lists, time blocking, and project management tools. We discuss how these methods can enhance productivity and efficiency.

CHAPTER 10: DELEGATION AND OUTSOURCING

Recognizing that we can't do everything ourselves is crucial for valuing our time. We discuss the importance of delegation and outsourcing tasks that are not essential or can be handled more efficiently by others. We provide guidance on how to delegate effectively and leverage resources.

CHAPTER 11: SAYING NO

Learning to say no is a skill that allows us to protect our time and focus on what truly matters. In this chapter, we discuss the importance of setting boundaries and assertively declining tasks and commitments that do not align with our priorities.

CHAPTER 12: TIME BLOCKING TECHNIQUES

Time blocking is a powerful technique for allocating specific time slots to different activities. We explore different time blocking methods, such as the **Pomodoro** Technique, and discuss how they can help us increase focus and productivity.

CHAPTER 13: MANAGING DISTRACTIONS

In this chapter, we delve deeper into managing distractions. We discuss techniques for creating an optimal work environment, minimizing interruptions, and developing focus and concentration skills to make the most of our time.

CHAPTER 14: EFFICIENT COMMUNICATION

Communication plays a vital role in how we utilize our time. We explore strategies for effective communication, including setting clear expectations, using concise and focused messages, and utilizing technology to streamline communication processes.

CHAPTER 15: HEALTHY WORK-LIFE BALANCE

Valuing our time extends beyond work-related activities. We emphasize the importance of maintaining a healthy work-life balance and discuss strategies for prioritizing personal time, self-care, and nurturing relationships.

CHAPTER 16: MINDFULNESS AND TIME AWARENESS

Mindfulness practices can help us cultivate a deeper appreciation for the present moment and develop a heightened awareness of how we use our time. In this chapter, we explore mindfulness techniques and their impact on time perception and management.

CHAPTER 17: MAXIMIZING PRODUCTIVITY

In this chapter, we discuss strategies for maximizing productivity. We explore techniques such as batching similar tasks, leveraging technology tools, and fostering a productive mindset to accomplish more in less time.

CHAPTER 18: THE POWER OF HABITS

Habits shape our daily routines and significantly impact how we utilize our time. We delve into the science of habit formation and discuss how implementing positive habits can lead to more efficient time management.

CHAPTER 19: MANAGING STRESS AND BURNOUT

Stress and burnout can derail our ability to value and manage our time effectively. We explore techniques for stress management, self-care practices, and strategies for preventing burnout to ensure sustainable time management.

CHAPTER 20: LEARNING TO RELAX

Relaxation is essential for recharging our energy and maintaining productivity. We discuss the benefits of relaxation techniques such as meditation, mindfulness, and hobbies, and how they contribute to better time management.

CHAPTER 21: FLEXIBILITY AND ADAPTABILITY

In today's fast-paced world, flexibility and adaptability are crucial skills for navigating time constraints. We discuss the importance of embracing change, adjusting plans when necessary, and cultivating a growth mindset to optimize our use of time.

CHAPTER 22: THE IMPACT OF TECHNOLOGY

Technology has transformed how we interact with time. In this chapter, we explore the benefits and challenges of technology in time management and discuss strategies for leveraging technology tools to enhance productivity while avoiding its potential pitfalls.

CHAPTER 23: CONTINUOUS IMPROVEMENT

Valuing our time is an ongoing process of self-reflection and improvement. We discuss the concept of continuous improvement and provide guidance on evaluating and refining our time management strategies to achieve optimal results.

CHAPTER 24: TEACHING TIME MANAGEMENT SKILLS

Time management is a valuable skill to pass on to others. We discuss the importance of teaching time management skills to children, students, and colleagues, and provide tips for effectively sharing our knowledge and experiences.

CHAPTER 25: CONCLUSION

In this final chapter, we summarize the key concepts covered throughout the book. We emphasize the importance of valuing our time, provide a call to action for implementing the strategies discussed, and leave readers with a lasting reminder to make the most of their limited

CHAPTER 1: INTRODUCTION

Time is a precious and finite resource, yet it often slips through our fingers unnoticed. We live in a world where everything seems to move at an accelerated pace, demanding our attention and stretching us thin. In this book, "It's Limited: Value Your Time," we embark on a journey to explore the significance of time, its limitations, and the art of managing it effectively.

Each passing moment brings us closer to the inevitable reality that time cannot be reclaimed. It is a non-renewable resource, a currency with which we purchase experiences, accomplishments, and the fulfillment of our aspirations. The way we choose to value and utilize this limited resource ultimately shapes the course of our lives.

The purpose of this book is to help you cultivate a deeper understanding and appreciation for the value of time. By exploring various concepts, strategies, and techniques, we aim to empower you to make conscious choices about how you allocate your time. We believe that by mastering the art of time management, you can create a more fulfilling and purpose-driven life.

In this introductory chapter, we lay the foundation for our exploration by discussing the nature of time and its perception. We delve into the philosophical and scientific theories surrounding time, as well as the impact of our subjective experience on its passage. By gaining a deeper understanding of time itself, we can begin to appreciate its true worth.

Time is a construct that governs our existence, yet it is an elusive concept. Philosophers and scientists have long grappled with the nature of time, leading to a myriad of theories and perspectives. From Aristotle's linear view of time to Einstein's theory of relativity, these ideas have shaped our understanding of the temporal dimension in which we live.

Furthermore, our perception of time plays a pivotal role in how we interact with it. We have all experienced moments that seem to fly by in an instant, while others drag on seemingly forever. The psychology behind our perception of time is a fascinating subject that can shed light on why certain activities feel more rewarding or draining, and how we can manipulate our perception to make the most of our time.

Recognizing the intrinsic value of time is paramount to embracing effective time management. Every decision we make involves a trade-off, an opportunity cost that requires us to sacrifice one activity in favor of another. By understanding the concept of opportunity cost and the potential impact of our choices, we become more intentional in our time allocation.

Moreover, valuing time extends beyond a mere appreciation of its worth. It entails setting priorities, establishing meaningful goals, and making conscious decisions about how we spend our moments. By recognizing that time is a limited resource, we gain a sense of urgency and motivation to make the most of it.

Throughout this book, we will explore a range of strategies and techniques to help you manage your time more effectively. From setting priorities and goal setting to overcoming procrastination and managing distractions, we will provide practical tools and insights to guide you on your journey towards optimizing your use of time.

However, it is important to note that time management is not a one-size-fits-all approach. What works for one person may not work for another. Therefore, we encourage you to approach this book with an open mind, ready to adapt and tailor the strategies to your unique circumstances and preferences. It is through experimentation and reflection that you will discover the most effective ways to value and manage your time.

As we embark on this exploration together, we invite you to reflect on your current relationship with time. Are you making conscious choices about how you spend your moments? Are you utilizing your time in alignment with your values and goals? By embarking on this journey of self-discovery and growth, you are taking the first step towards a more fulfilling and purposeful life.

In the subsequent chapters, we will delve into specific aspects of time management, providing practical guidance, actionable tips, and real-life examples. We will explore topics such as effective planning techniques, delegation and outsourcing, managing distractions, and cultivating a healthy work-life balance. Each chapter will build upon the previous one, offering a comprehensive roadmap towards optimizing your use of time.

So, let us embark on this transformative journey together. Let us delve into the realm of time, unlock its secrets, and harness its power to create a life filled with purpose, accomplishment, and fulfillment. Remember, time is limited, but its potential is boundless. It is up to us to value and make the most of it.

CHAPTER 2: UNDERSTANDING TIME

Time is a fundamental aspect of our existence, yet its nature remains elusive and mysterious. In this chapter, we delve into the concept of time, exploring its philosophical and scientific dimensions, and seeking a deeper understanding of its influence on our lives.

THE NATURE OF TIME

Time is a construct that permeates every aspect of our lives. It is the fabric upon which our experiences unfold and our memories are formed. But what exactly is time? Philosophers and thinkers throughout history have grappled with this question, resulting in various theories and perspectives.

One of the earliest theories about time is attributed to Aristotle, who proposed that time is the measurement of change. According to Aristotle, time is inseparable from the physical world and is contingent upon events unfolding and things coming into being and passing away.

In contrast, Immanuel Kant argued that time is not an inherent property of the external world but a fundamental framework of human perception. He posited that time is a subjective concept that allows us to make sense of our experiences and organize them in a coherent manner.

These differing perspectives highlight the complexity of understanding time. It is both an external force that governs our existence and a subjective construct through which we perceive and make sense of the world.

THE ARROW OF TIME

Another intriguing aspect of time is its directional nature, often referred to as the "arrow of time." Time has an inherent flow, moving from the past through the present and into the future. This unidirectional flow is a fundamental aspect of our experience, shaping our perception and influencing our decision-making.

The concept of the arrow of time is closely tied to the second law of thermodynamics, which states that the entropy, or disorder, of a closed system tends to increase over time. This increase in entropy aligns with our subjective experience of time, where the past is characterized by order and the future by uncertainty and increasing complexity.

The arrow of time also manifests in our memories. We can remember events that have occurred in the past, but we cannot predict with certainty what the future holds. This asymmetry between our ability to recall the past and our inability to foresee the future further underscores the directional nature of time.

THE RELATIVITY OF TIME

In the early 20th century, Albert Einstein revolutionized our understanding of time with his theory of relativity. According to Einstein, time is not an absolute, constant entity but a dynamic and malleable dimension that can be influenced by various factors.

Einstein's theory of special relativity introduced the concept of time dilation, which states that time can pass differently for different observers depending on their relative motion.

This phenomenon has been experimentally verified and has profound implications for our perception of time.

Furthermore, Einstein's theory of general relativity proposed that gravity can also affect the passage of time. In regions of high gravitational fields, time can slow down relative to regions with lower gravitational fields. This effect, known as gravitational time dilation, has been observed in experiments and confirmed by the synchronization of atomic clocks at different altitudes.

The relativity of time challenges our intuition about its universality and sheds light on the interconnectedness of time, space, and matter. It highlights the intricate relationship between the physical world and the perception of time, blurring the boundaries between objective and subjective experiences.

THE PSYCHOLOGICAL PERCEPTION OF TIME

Beyond the philosophical and scientific dimensions, our perception of time is heavily influenced by psychological factors. We often experience time as subjective, with some moments flying by while others seem to drag on indefinitely.

Psychological research has identified several factors that contribute to our perception of time. One such factor is attention. When we are fully engaged and immersed in an activity, time tends to pass quickly. Conversely, when we are bored or disengaged, time can feel sluggish and prolonged.

Emotional states also influence our perception of time. In moments of excitement or anticipation, time appears to accelerate, whereas in moments of stress or boredom, it may stretch and feel interminable. This emotional time dilation showcases the intricate interplay between our mental and emotional states and our experience of time.

Cultural and societal influences also shape our perception of time. Different cultures have varying perspectives on the pace of life, punctuality, and the value placed on time. These cultural norms and expectations can significantly impact individuals' subjective experience and attitudes towards time.

Understanding the psychological aspects of time perception empowers us to harness our perception for optimal time management. By creating conditions that promote engagement, flow, and positive emotions, we can shape our perception of time and make the most of each passing moment.

THE VALUE OF TIME AWARENESS

Developing time awareness is an essential aspect of valuing and managing our time effectively. By cultivating an acute sense of the passage of time, we can make informed decisions about how we allocate our limited resource.

Time awareness involves being present in the moment, actively engaging with the task at hand, and developing a heightened sensitivity to the flow of time. It requires us to be mindful of our choices and actions, recognizing the opportunity costs associated with each decision.

Furthermore, time awareness helps us identify patterns and tendencies in how we utilize our time. By reflecting on our habits and behaviors, we can gain insights into areas where we may be wasting time or engaging in unproductive activities. This self-awareness lays the foundation for effective time management.

In the subsequent chapters, we will explore strategies and techniques for enhancing time awareness, managing our perception of time, and making conscious choices about how we utilize this limited resource. By embracing a deeper understanding of time and its nuances, we can unlock the keys to valuing and optimizing our use of time.

In Conclusion Time is a multifaceted concept that transcends physical, philosophical, and psychological boundaries. It is both an objective force governing our existence and a subjective construct influenced by our perception and experiences. Understanding the nature of time and our relationship with it is vital for cultivating a mindful and purposeful approach to time management.

As we journey further into this book, we will delve into practical strategies for managing time effectively, setting priorities, overcoming procrastination, and cultivating a healthy work-life balance. By combining these practical tools with a deeper understanding of the nature of time, you will be equipped with the knowledge and skills to value and make the most of your limited time.

CHAPTER 3: THE VALUE OF TIME

Time is an intangible yet invaluable resource that permeates every aspect of our lives. It is limited, finite, and non-renewable. In this chapter, we delve into the concept of time as a valuable asset, exploring the profound impact it has on our lives and the importance of recognizing and appreciating its worth.

THE INTRINSIC VALUE OF TIME

Time holds intrinsic value that extends far beyond its utilitarian purpose. It is a precious commodity that cannot be bought, stored, or replenished. Each passing moment is an opportunity for growth, learning, and connection. By recognizing the inherent value of time, we are compelled to make the most of every fleeting second.

The value of time lies in its potential. It offers us the chance to pursue our passions, achieve our goals, and experience the richness of life. It is through the effective utilization of time that we can make significant progress, create meaningful relationships, and leave a lasting impact on the world.

OPPORTUNITY COST

The Price of Time Every decision we make involves a trade-off, an opportunity cost that requires us to sacrifice one activity in favor of another. Time is the currency with which we pay this cost. When we choose to spend time on one endeavor, we forego the opportunity to allocate it to another.

Understanding the concept of opportunity cost is crucial for valuing our time. It compels us to evaluate the potential benefits and drawbacks of each choice and make informed decisions about how we allocate our limited resource. By recognizing that time is a valuable and finite asset, we become more intentional in our choices and ensure that we prioritize activities that align with our goals and values.

THE PRICELESS MOMENTS OF LIFE

Time grants us the opportunity to experience the richness and beauty of life. It is during the moments we cherish, the milestones we celebrate, and the connections we forge that the true value of time becomes apparent.

Think of the joy of spending quality time with loved ones, the sense of accomplishment upon achieving a long-held goal, or the serenity found in moments of solitude and self-reflection. These priceless moments are made possible by the gift of time. They remind us of the fleeting nature of existence and the importance of cherishing each passing moment.

REGRET AND THE IMPORTANCE OF SEIZING THE MOMENT

Regret is a poignant reminder of the value of time. When we reflect on missed opportunities, unfulfilled dreams, or moments squandered, we recognize the irrevocable nature of time and the weight of our choices.

Regret can serve as a catalyst for change. It urges us to seize the moment, to make the most of the time we have, and to live with intention and purpose. By learning from past regrets and embracing a proactive approach to time management, we can minimize future regrets and create a life filled with meaningful experiences.

TIME AS A DRIVER OF SUCCESS

The effective management of time is a fundamental pillar of success. It empowers us to allocate our resources strategically, make progress towards our goals, and accomplish more with less effort.

Time management skills are highly sought after in both personal and professional domains. Individuals who can effectively prioritize, plan, and execute tasks are more likely to achieve their objectives, meet deadlines, and experience a greater sense of accomplishment.

Moreover, valuing and managing time demonstrates respect for oneself and others. It reflects a commitment to efficiency, productivity, and a strong work ethic. By honoring our time and the time of those around us, we create a culture that fosters growth, collaboration, and achievement.

THE ILLUSION OF INFINITE TIME

One of the greatest fallacies we often fall prey to is the illusion of infinite time. We tend to operate under the assumption that there will always be more time in the future, leading us to postpone important tasks, delay pursuing our dreams, or neglect spending quality time with loved ones.

However, time is a finite resource, and none of us know how much we truly have. Embracing the reality of time's limitations is a catalyst for action. It compels us to prioritize what truly matters, to eliminate procrastination, and to make deliberate choices that align with our values and goals.

CULTIVATING A MINDSET OF TIME APPRECIATION

Appreciating the value of time requires a mindset shift. It involves consciously choosing to view time as a precious and finite resource, rather than taking it for granted. By embracing a mindset of time appreciation, we can foster a deeper sense of gratitude, urgency, and responsibility towards how we allocate our time.

Practicing gratitude for the time we have is a powerful way to cultivate this mindset. Each day, we can take a moment to reflect on the gift of time and express gratitude for the opportunities it affords us. This simple practice can create a ripple effect, instilling a sense of purpose, motivation, and fulfillment in our daily lives.

THE IMPACT OF VALUING TIME

Valuing time has far-reaching implications that extend beyond personal fulfillment. When we recognize the worth of time, we become more conscientious members of society, mindful of how our choices and actions impact others.

Valuing time leads to enhanced productivity and efficiency, enabling us to contribute our skills and talents in meaningful ways. It also fosters stronger relationships, as we prioritize quality interactions and invest time in nurturing connections with loved ones.

Furthermore, valuing time helps us develop a greater sense of self-awareness and self-respect. By consciously managing our time, we demonstrate a commitment to personal growth, self-care, and the pursuit of our aspirations.

In Conclusion Time is a precious and limited resource that holds immeasurable value. By recognizing and appreciating its worth, we unlock the key to a more purposeful and fulfilling life. Valuing time empowers us to make conscious choices, allocate our resources strategically, and seize the opportunities that come our way.

In the subsequent chapters, we will delve into practical strategies and techniques for effective time management. We will explore topics such as setting priorities, goal setting, overcoming procrastination, and managing distractions. By combining these practical tools with a deep appreciation for the value of time, you will be equipped with the knowledge and mindset necessary to optimize your use of this finite resource.

CHAPTER 4: SETTING PRIORITIES

E ffective time management begins with setting priorities. In a world filled with endless demands and distractions, it is crucial to identify and focus on the tasks and activities that truly matter. In this chapter, we explore the art of setting priorities and provide practical strategies for allocating your time in alignment with your goals and values.

THE IMPORTANCE OF PRIORITIZATION

Prioritization is the process of determining the relative importance of tasks, activities, and goals. It allows us to allocate our time, energy, and resources to the most significant and impactful areas of our lives. Without clear priorities, we risk getting caught up in trivial pursuits and losing sight of what truly matters.

Setting priorities is particularly essential in today's fast-paced and information-saturated world. With countless demands competing for our attention, it is easy to become overwhelmed and lose focus. By intentionally setting priorities, we regain control over our time and ensure that we are investing it in activities that align with our values and goals.

THE EISENHOWER MATRIX

One popular framework for setting priorities is the Eisenhower Matrix, also known as the Urgent-Important Matrix. Developed by President Dwight D. Eisenhower, this tool provides a systematic approach to categorizing tasks based on their urgency and importance.

The matrix divides tasks into four quadrants:

Quadrant 1: Urgent and Important - These are tasks that require immediate attention and have a significant impact on your goals and well-being. Examples include meeting crucial deadlines, handling emergencies, and addressing pressing personal or professional issues.

Quadrant 2: Important but Not Urgent - These tasks contribute to long-term goals, personal growth, and well-being but may not have immediate deadlines. Quadrant 2 tasks include strategic planning, skill development, relationship building, and self-care activities. This quadrant is often the most neglected but holds tremendous value in fostering personal and professional growth.

Quadrant 3: Urgent but Not Important - Tasks in this quadrant are often distractions and interruptions that demand immediate attention but do not contribute significantly to your long-term goals. They may include unnecessary meetings, non-essential emails or phone calls, and trivial tasks that can be delegated or eliminated.

Quadrant 4: Not Urgent and Not Important - These tasks are low-value activities that offer little or no benefit. They often involve time-wasting activities like excessive social media use, mindless browsing, or indulging in unproductive habits. Minimizing time spent in this quadrant is essential for effective time management.

By using the Eisenhower Matrix, you can gain clarity on how to prioritize tasks and make informed decisions about where to invest your time and energy.

IDENTIFYING CORE VALUES AND GOALS

To set meaningful priorities, it is important to identify your core values and long-term goals. Your values are the guiding principles that define what is important to you and shape your decision-making process. By aligning your priorities with your values, you ensure that your time is spent on activities that bring you fulfillment and contribute to your sense of purpose.

Take time for self-reflection and identify the values that resonate with you. Is it personal growth, family, health, creativity, or making a difference in the world? Once you have a clear understanding of your values, you can set goals that align with them. Goals provide a roadmap for where you want to be and enable you to allocate your time and resources accordingly.

THE SMART GOAL FRAMEWORK

A widely used framework for setting effective goals is the SMART acronym:

Specific: Clearly define your goal. Instead of a vague objective like "improve fitness," make it specific by stating "run a half-marathon within six months."

Measurable: Establish concrete criteria for measuring progress and success. In the example of running a half-marathon, you can track the number of miles run per week or monitor improvements in your race times.

Achievable: Ensure that your goal is realistic and attainable. Set challenging but reachable targets that motivate you to push yourself while acknowledging your current capabilities and resources.

Relevant: Assess the relevance of your goal to your values and long-term objectives. Ask yourself if the goal aligns with your priorities and contributes to your overall sense of fulfillment and purpose.

Time-bound: Set a deadline or timeframe for achieving your goal. Having a clear time frame creates a sense of urgency and helps you plan and allocate your time effectively.

By following the SMART goal framework, you can ensure that your goals are well-defined, actionable, and aligned with your priorities.

THE 80/20 RULE (PARETO PRINCIPLE)

The Pareto Principle, commonly known as the 80/20 rule, suggests that 80% of your outcomes are derived from 20% of your efforts. Applied to time management, this principle emphasizes the importance of focusing on the most impactful and high-value tasks that yield the greatest results.

Identify the tasks and activities that contribute most significantly to your desired outcomes and prioritize them. By focusing your time and energy on the vital few, you can maximize your productivity and make substantial progress towards your goals.

EVALUATING URGENCY AND IMPORTANCE

When determining priorities, it is crucial to evaluate the urgency and importance of each task or activity. Urgency refers to how soon a task needs to be completed, while importance relates to the impact the task has on your goals and values.

Avoid falling into the trap of confusing urgency with importance. Not all urgent tasks are essential, and not all important tasks are urgent. By evaluating each task's true significance, you can avoid the tendency to prioritize urgent but unimportant activities over those with long-term value.

LEARNING TO SAY NO

Setting priorities often requires the ability to say no to activities that do not align with your goals and values. Many of us struggle with the fear of disappointing others or missing out on opportunities. However, saying no is essential for protecting your time and maintaining focus on your highest priorities.

Practice assertiveness and learn to decline requests or commitments that do not align with your priorities. Communicate your boundaries and explain your reasons for declining. Remember, saying no to the non-essential allows you to say yes to what truly matters.

REASSESSING AND ADJUSTING PRIORITIES

Setting priorities is not a one-time exercise. It is an ongoing process that requires regular reassessment and adjustment. As circumstances change and new opportunities arise, it is essential to review and refine your priorities to ensure they remain aligned with your evolving goals and values.

Schedule regular check-ins with yourself to evaluate your progress, reflect on your priorities, and make any necessary adjustments. This practice enables you to stay on track, adapt to new challenges, and make the most effective use of your time.

In Conclusion Setting priorities is a cornerstone of effective time management. By clarifying your values, setting SMART goals, using frameworks like the Eisenhower Matrix, and evaluating urgency and importance, you can ensure that your time is allocated to activities that align with your long-term objectives and bring you closer to a fulfilled and purposeful life.

In the next chapter, we will explore the process of goal setting in more detail, providing practical strategies for defining and pursuing meaningful goals. By combining the art of setting priorities with effective goal setting techniques, you will gain the tools necessary to make the most of your limited time and create a life filled with purpose and accomplishment.

CHAPTER 5: GOAL SETTING

Setting goals is a powerful and transformative process that enables us to direct our time, energy, and resources towards meaningful outcomes. In this chapter, we delve into the art of goal setting, exploring the importance of clear objectives, the benefits of setting goals, and providing practical strategies for defining and pursuing goals that align with your values and aspirations.

THE POWER OF GOAL SETTING

Goals serve as beacons of light, guiding us towards our desired destinations. They provide focus, motivation, and a sense of direction. By setting goals, we create a roadmap for our actions and allocate our time and resources intentionally.

Goal setting has been studied extensively in various fields, including psychology, business, and personal development. Research consistently demonstrates the positive impact of goal setting on performance, productivity, and overall well-being. It helps us channel our efforts effectively, enhance self-confidence, and create a sense of purpose and fulfillment.

THE CHARACTERISTICS OF EFFECTIVE GOALS

To ensure that goals are meaningful and impactful, they should possess certain characteristics. Effective goals are:

Specific: A goal should be clear and well-defined. Vague or ambiguous goals make it challenging to track progress or determine when they have been achieved. Specific goals provide a target to aim for and enable you to create actionable plans.

Measurable: Goals should be measurable, allowing you to assess progress and success objectively. By establishing specific criteria for measuring progress, you can track your advancement and stay motivated throughout the process.

Achievable: While goals should stretch you and push you out of your comfort zone, they should also be realistic and attainable. Setting excessively challenging or unrealistic goals can lead to frustration and demotivation. Strive for goals that are within your reach with effort and dedication.

Relevant: Goals should be aligned with your values, long-term objectives, and overall vision for your life. They should contribute to your sense of fulfillment and purpose, ensuring that the efforts invested in pursuing them are meaningful and worthwhile.

Time-bound: Goals need to have a clear time frame or deadline. Setting a specific time frame creates a sense of urgency, provides a structure for planning and execution, and helps you allocate your time effectively.

By incorporating these characteristics into your goal-setting process, you enhance the clarity, motivation, and likelihood of achieving your objectives.

TYPES OF GOALS

Goals can be categorized into different types based on their nature and time frame. Here are some common types of goals:

Short-term goals: These goals typically span a few weeks to a few months and focus on relatively immediate outcomes. Short-term goals help you make progress incrementally, maintain momentum, and build confidence.

Long-term goals: Long-term goals cover a more extended time frame, often spanning years. They are usually significant aspirations that require sustained effort and commitment. Long-term goals provide a sense of direction and enable you to align your actions and decisions accordingly.

Process goals: Process goals focus on the actions, behaviors, or habits necessary to achieve desired outcomes. They are within your control and are crucial for building consistency and progress. Examples of process goals include exercising three times a week, reading for 30 minutes daily, or practicing a skill for a set amount of time each day.

Outcome goals: Outcome goals refer to the specific results or achievements you aim to accomplish. They represent the ultimate outcomes you desire. While outcome goals are essential, it is crucial to focus on the process goals that will lead to these outcomes. By prioritizing the actions and behaviors within your control, you can make steady progress towards your desired outcomes.

THE SMARTER GOAL FRAMEWORK

Building upon the SMART framework discussed earlier, the SMARTER goal framework adds two additional components: Evaluation and Revision.

Specific: Ensure that your goal is well-defined, clear, and specific.

Measurable: Establish criteria to measure progress and success objectively.

Achievable: Set goals that are realistic and within your reach with effort and dedication.

Relevant: Align your goals with your values, aspirations, and long-term vision.

Time-bound: Set a specific time frame or deadline for achieving your goals.

Evaluated: Regularly assess your progress towards your goals and make adjustments as needed. Evaluation allows you to stay on track and make informed decisions about your strategies and actions.

Revised: Be open to revising your goals as circumstances change or new opportunities arise. Flexibility and adaptability are key to effective goal setting.

By incorporating evaluation and revision into your goal-setting process, you create a feedback loop that enables continuous improvement and alignment with your evolving aspirations.

BREAKING DOWN GOALS INTO MILESTONES AND ACTION STEPS

Large goals can often feel overwhelming, making it challenging to make progress. Breaking down goals into smaller milestones and actionable steps is a powerful technique for managing complexity, maintaining motivation, and tracking progress.

Milestones are significant checkpoints along the path to achieving your goals. They serve as indicators of progress and can provide a sense of accomplishment and momentum. By setting meaningful milestones, you create a roadmap that keeps you focused and enables you to celebrate smaller victories along the way.

Action steps are the specific tasks or activities that need to be completed to reach your milestones. They break down larger goals into manageable, actionable items. By outlining the necessary action steps, you provide yourself with a clear plan of action and ensure that you make consistent progress towards your desired outcomes.

VISUALIZING AND AFFIRMING GOALS

Visualization is a powerful technique that involves mentally picturing yourself achieving your goals. By vividly imagining the successful accomplishment of your objectives, you tap into the power of your subconscious mind and enhance motivation, focus, and belief in your ability to succeed.

Affirmations are positive statements that reinforce your belief in your ability to achieve your goals. By repeating affirmations regularly, you instill a sense of confidence and resilience. Affirmations can help counteract self-doubt, boost self-esteem, and maintain a positive mindset throughout the goal pursuit process.

OVERCOMING OBSTACLES AND ADAPTING TO CHALLENGES

Goal pursuit is rarely a linear and obstacle-free journey. Challenges, setbacks, and unexpected circumstances are inevitable. It is essential to anticipate and prepare for potential obstacles to stay resilient and maintain progress.

Develop contingency plans for potential challenges and setbacks. Consider alternative approaches, resources, or strategies that can help you overcome obstacles and keep moving forward. Embrace a growth mindset that views challenges as opportunities for learning and growth, rather than as insurmountable roadblocks.

Adaptability is a crucial skill in goal setting. As circumstances change or new opportunities arise, be open to adjusting your goals and strategies. Flexibility allows you to seize new possibilities and ensures that your goals remain relevant and aligned with your evolving aspirations.

CELEBRATING MILESTONES AND REFLECTING ON PROGRESS

As you achieve milestones and make progress towards your goals, take time to celebrate and acknowledge your accomplishments. Celebrating milestones provides a boost of motivation, reinforces positive habits, and creates a sense of satisfaction and fulfillment.

Reflection is another important practice in goal setting. Regularly assess your progress, evaluate the effectiveness of your strategies, and reflect on what you have learned along the way. Reflection allows you to make necessary adjustments, identify areas for improvement, and refine your approach to goal pursuit.

In Conclusion Goal setting is a transformative process that empowers you to make the most of your limited time. By setting clear and meaningful goals, incorporating the SMARTER framework, breaking down goals into milestones and action steps, and adapting to challenges, you can create a roadmap for success.

In the coming chapters, we will explore practical strategies for overcoming procrastination and enhancing productivity. By combining effective goal setting techniques with strategies for action and execution, you will gain the tools necessary to maximize your use of time and achieve your desired outcomes.

CHAPTER 6:
TIME AUDIT

A time audit is a powerful tool for gaining insights into how you currently allocate your time and identifying areas for improvement. In this chapter, we explore the concept of a time audit, its benefits, and provide practical strategies for conducting a thorough assessment of your time usage. By conducting a time audit, you can make informed decisions about how to optimize your time and align it with your priorities and goals.

UNDERSTANDING THE TIME AUDIT

A time audit involves tracking and analyzing how you spend your time over a defined period. It provides an objective snapshot of how your time is currently allocated, allowing you to identify patterns, uncover time-wasting activities, and make conscious choices about how to use your time more effectively.

The purpose of a time audit is to gain awareness and insight into your time usage. It helps you answer questions such as:

How much time do you spend on different activities?

Are you allocating time in alignment with your priorities and goals?

What are your most time-consuming tasks and activities?

Are there any patterns or habits that hinder your productivity?

Are there any opportunities for optimizing your time allocation?

BENEFITS OF A TIME AUDIT

Conducting a time audit offers numerous benefits that can positively impact your productivity, efficiency, and overall well-being. Some of the key benefits include:

Increased self-awareness: A time audit provides a clear picture of how you currently spend your time. It helps you become aware of time-wasting activities, unproductive habits, and areas where you can make improvements.

Identification of time leaks: A time audit helps you identify time leaks—small pockets of time that are often wasted or underutilized. By identifying these leaks, you can reclaim valuable minutes and redirect them towards activities that align with your goals and priorities.

Enhanced productivity: Understanding how you currently allocate your time allows you to optimize your schedule and focus on high-value tasks. By eliminating or reducing time spent on low-value activities, you can increase productivity and accomplish more in less time.

Improved time management: A time audit enables you to make informed decisions about how to allocate your time more effectively. By recognizing patterns, identifying areas for improvement, and making adjustments, you can optimize your time management strategies.

Alignment with priorities: A time audit helps ensure that your time is spent on activities that align with your values and long-term goals. It enables you to evaluate whether your current time allocation reflects your priorities and make necessary adjustments.

CONDUCTING A TIME AUDIT

Conducting a time audit involves tracking and analyzing how

you spend your time. Here are practical steps to conduct a comprehensive time audit:

Step 1: Define the time period: Determine the duration of your time audit. It can range from a few days to a week or even a month, depending on the level of detail you desire.

Step 2: Select a tracking method: Choose a method to track your time. There are various options available, including:

Manual tracking: Use a notebook or a time-tracking app to record your activities and the time spent on each.

Digital tools: Utilize time-tracking apps or productivity software that automatically track your activities based on your device usage.

Select a method that suits your preferences and lifestyle, ensuring it is convenient and easy to use consistently throughout the time audit period.

Step 3: Track your time diligently: Start tracking your activities from the moment you wake up until you go to bed. Be diligent and record your activities as accurately as possible. Include details such as the activity, start time, end time, and any relevant notes or observations.

Step 4: Categorize your activities: After the tracking period, categorize your activities into different groups or categories. For example, you might have categories such as work-related tasks, personal activities, leisure time, household chores, and so on. This categorization allows you to gain a broader understanding of how you spend your time.

Step 5: Analyze your time usage: Review the data from your time audit and analyze how you allocate your time. Look for patterns, time leaks, and areas where you spend an excessive amount of time on low-value activities. Identify any discrepancies between your time allocation and your priorities or goals.

Step 6: Reflect and make adjustments: Reflect on the insights gained from your time audit. Evaluate the effectiveness of your time allocation and identify areas where changes can be made. Make adjustments to your schedule, habits, and priorities based on the findings of your time audit.

TIME AUDIT STRATEGIES AND TIPS

To conduct a thorough and effective time audit, consider the following strategies and tips:

Be consistent: Ensure that you track your time consistently throughout the audit period. Capture both work-related and personal activities to gain a holistic view of your time usage.

Be honest: Record your activities truthfully, without bias or judgment. The purpose of the time audit is to gain accurate insights, so honesty is essential.

Include all activities: Capture both planned and unplanned activities. This includes breaks, interruptions, and time spent on social media or other distractions.

Use technology: Leverage technology tools such as time-tracking apps or productivity software to automate the process and minimize manual effort.

Take note of emotions: Alongside tracking your activities, note how you feel during different tasks. This can help identify patterns where certain activities drain your energy or bring you joy and satisfaction.

Evaluate your energy levels: Make a note of your energy levels throughout the day. This can help you identify optimal times for focusing on high-priority tasks that require concentration and creativity.

Review weekly and monthly trends: Look for patterns and trends in your time usage over a week or month. This will help you identify recurring patterns and make long-term adjustments to your schedule.

APPLYING INSIGHTS FROM THE TIME AUDIT

The true value of a time audit lies in applying the insights gained to make meaningful changes. Here are some ways you can apply the insights from your time audit:

Eliminate or delegate low-value activities: Identify time-consuming tasks or activities that contribute little value to your goals or well-being. Eliminate them if possible, or delegate them to others if appropriate.

Optimize high-value activities: Look for ways to streamline and optimize tasks that are essential and high-value. Identify opportunities for automation, batch processing, or outsourcing to free up time for other activities.

Set boundaries and establish routines: Use the insights from your time audit to establish boundaries and routines that support your priorities. Create dedicated blocks of time for important tasks, minimize distractions, and establish consistent routines that promote productivity and focus.

Time blocking and scheduling: Incorporate time blocking techniques into your schedule to allocate specific time slots for different tasks or activities. This helps ensure that you have dedicated time for important activities and prevents time leakage.

Focus on energy management: Take note of the times when your energy levels are highest and align your most important or challenging tasks during these periods. Prioritize activities that require concentration, creativity, or problem-solving during your peak energy times.

Practice self-discipline and time management techniques: Apply effective time management techniques such as the Pomodoro Technique (working in focused bursts with timed breaks), prioritizing tasks using the Eisenhower Matrix, or utilizing productivity apps and tools to manage your time effectively.

EMBRACING A CONTINUOUS IMPROVEMENT MINDSET

A time audit is not a one-time exercise but a continuous practice of self-reflection and improvement. Embrace a mindset of continuous improvement, regularly reassessing your time allocation, and making adjustments as needed. As your priorities and goals evolve, adapt your time management strategies to ensure that your time usage remains aligned with what truly matters to you.

In Conclusion Conducting a time audit provides invaluable insights into how you currently use your time and allows you to make informed decisions about optimizing it. By identifying time leaks, aligning your time allocation with priorities, and making necessary adjustments, you can maximize the value of your limited time and move closer to your goals. In the next chapter, we will explore strategies for overcoming procrastination and improving productivity, empowering you to make the most of your time.

CHAPTER 7: OVERCOMING PROCRASTINATION

Procrastination is a common challenge that plagues many individuals, preventing them from making the most of their time and achieving their goals. In this chapter, we explore the causes and consequences of procrastination and provide practical strategies for overcoming this detrimental habit. By mastering techniques to combat procrastination, you can regain control of your time and boost your productivity.

UNDERSTANDING PROCRASTINATION

Procrastination refers to the act of delaying or postponing tasks or activities that require immediate attention. It is often characterized by the tendency to engage in unproductive or irrelevant activities in place of important tasks. While procrastination may provide temporary relief or comfort, it ultimately leads to stress, missed deadlines, and decreased productivity.

THE CAUSES OF PROCRASTINATION

Procrastination can stem from various underlying causes. Understanding these causes can help you identify the root of your procrastination tendencies and develop effective strategies to overcome them. Some common causes of procrastination include:

Fear of failure: The fear of making mistakes or falling short of expectations can lead to procrastination. When the fear of failure outweighs the motivation to succeed, individuals may avoid taking action altogether.

Perfectionism: Perfectionists often struggle with procrastination due to the desire to achieve flawless results. The fear of not meeting high standards can lead to delays in starting or completing tasks.

Lack of motivation: When tasks lack intrinsic motivation or fail to align with personal interests and values, it can be challenging to muster the drive necessary to initiate or complete them.

Overwhelm and lack of clarity: Feeling overwhelmed by the magnitude or complexity of a task can result in procrastination. Uncertainty about where to start or how to proceed can paralyze individuals, leading to inaction.

Lack of discipline and self-regulation: Difficulty in self-regulation, time management, and prioritization can contribute to procrastination. Without clear structures and strategies in place, individuals may struggle to stay focused and complete tasks on time.

THE CONSEQUENCES OF PROCRASTINATION

Procrastination has numerous negative consequences that extend beyond missed deadlines and uncompleted tasks. Some common consequences include:

Increased stress and anxiety: Procrastination often leads to heightened stress levels as deadlines loom closer and tasks accumulate. The constant pressure of unfinished work can contribute to anxiety and a sense of overwhelm.

Decline in productivity: Engaging in unproductive activities instead of important tasks hinders productivity. Procrastination diminishes the time available for meaningful work and can result in a decreased output of high-quality work.

Impaired reputation and credibility: Consistently failing to meet deadlines or deliver on promises can damage your professional or personal reputation. Others may perceive you as unreliable or untrustworthy, impacting your relationships and opportunities.

Missed opportunities: Procrastination can result in missed opportunities, both professionally and personally. By delaying action, you may miss out on valuable chances for growth, advancement, or meaningful experiences.

Regret and dissatisfaction: Procrastination often leads to regret and dissatisfaction. Reflecting on wasted time and missed opportunities can erode self-esteem and hinder personal growth.

STRATEGIES FOR OVERCOMING PROCRASTINATION

Overcoming procrastination requires conscious effort, self-awareness, and the implementation of effective strategies. Here are practical techniques to help you combat procrastination and make the most of your time:

Set clear goals and deadlines: Establish specific and achievable goals, accompanied by realistic deadlines. Clear goals provide focus and motivation, while deadlines create a sense of urgency and structure.

Break tasks into smaller steps: Large tasks can feel overwhelming, leading to procrastination. Break them down into smaller, more manageable steps to make them less intimidating. Focus on completing one step at a time, gradually building momentum.

Prioritize tasks: Use techniques like the Eisenhower Matrix (discussed in Chapter 3) to identify and prioritize tasks based on urgency and importance. Tackle high-priority tasks first to prevent them from being postponed or overlooked.

Create a structured schedule: Develop a structured schedule that outlines specific time blocks for different tasks and activities. Allocate dedicated time for focused work, breaks, and leisure activities. Stick to the schedule to cultivate discipline and avoid succumbing to distractions.

Utilize time-management techniques: Explore various time-management techniques to improve focus and productivity. Techniques such as the Pomodoro Technique (working in focused intervals with short breaks), time blocking, and the Two-Minute Rule (if a task takes less than two minutes, do it immediately) can help overcome procrastination tendencies.

Combat perfectionism: Recognize that perfectionism can hinder progress and contribute to procrastination. Embrace a growth mindset, acknowledging that mistakes are part of the learning process. Set realistic expectations and aim for progress rather than perfection.

Find intrinsic motivation: Connect tasks to your values, goals, or personal interests to increase intrinsic motivation. Identify the benefits and positive outcomes associated with completing each task, reinforcing the purpose behind your actions.

Manage distractions: Identify and minimize potential distractions in your environment. Put your phone on silent or in a different room, block distracting websites or apps, and create a clutter-free workspace to reduce visual distractions.

Practice effective time management: Develop effective time management habits, such as prioritizing tasks, setting deadlines, and creating to-do lists. Regularly review and update your task list to ensure it remains relevant and aligned with your goals.

Utilize accountability and support systems: Share your goals and deadlines with an accountability partner or mentor who can provide guidance and hold you accountable. Joining a study group, mastermind group, or hiring a coach can also provide the necessary support and motivation.

Celebrate progress and reward yourself: Acknowledge and celebrate each completed task or milestone. Rewarding yourself reinforces positive habits and provides a sense of accomplishment, encouraging you to continue taking action.

Cultivate self-discipline: Develop self-discipline by committing to follow through on your commitments and honoring deadlines. Practicing self-discipline strengthens your ability to resist procrastination and stay focused on important tasks.

DEVELOPING A PROACTIVE MINDSET

Overcoming procrastination requires a proactive mindset and a commitment to taking action. Adopt these principles to cultivate a proactive approach to your time management:

Take ownership of your time: Recognize that you have control over how you allocate your time. Accept responsibility for your actions and the consequences of procrastination.

Focus on progress, not perfection: Shift your focus from achieving perfect results to making consistent progress. Embrace a growth mindset and view challenges as opportunities for learning and improvement.

Embrace discomfort: Acknowledge that discomfort or resistance may arise when facing challenging tasks. Embrace the discomfort as a sign of growth and push through it to complete the task at hand.

Practice self-reflection: Regularly reflect on your habits, tendencies, and patterns related to procrastination. Identify triggers, emotional states, or environmental factors that contribute to procrastination. Use this self-awareness to develop strategies to counteract them.

Emphasize the present moment: Cultivate mindfulness and focus on the present moment. Avoid dwelling on past procrastination or worrying excessively about future tasks.

Direct your attention and energy towards the task at hand.

BUILDING LONG-TERM HABITS FOR SUCCESS

Overcoming procrastination is not a one-time event but a process of building long-term habits. Here are strategies for developing lasting habits that support productivity and time management:

Consistency: Commit to consistent action by practicing productive habits daily. Consistency reinforces positive behavior and helps solidify new habits.

Gradual improvement: Start small and gradually increase the intensity and duration of your productive habits. Aim for continuous improvement rather than sudden, unsustainable changes.

Reflection and adjustment: Regularly reflect on your progress and adjust your strategies as needed. Continuously assess the effectiveness of your time management techniques and make necessary adaptations.

Accountability and support: Seek accountability and support from peers, mentors, or coaches who can provide guidance and encouragement. Engaging with like-minded individuals can strengthen your commitment and motivation.

Persistence: Overcoming procrastination requires perseverance. Be prepared for setbacks and temporary lapses but remain dedicated to your goals. Persistence is key to long-term success.

EMBRACING THE VALUE OF TIME

Overcoming procrastination ultimately comes down to valuing your time and recognizing its limited nature. Embrace the understanding that time is a precious resource that can never be regained once lost. Cultivate gratitude for the time you have and commit to making the most of every moment.

In Conclusion Procrastination is a habit that can hinder productivity and prevent you from achieving your goals. By understanding the causes of procrastination, implementing effective strategies, and cultivating a proactive mindset, you can overcome this habit and optimize your time usage. In the next chapter, we will explore techniques for enhancing focus and concentration, enabling you to accomplish tasks more efficiently and effectively.

CHAPTER 8: AVOIDING TIME WASTERS

In today's fast-paced world, time wasters can easily infiltrate our lives, consuming valuable minutes and hindering our productivity. In this chapter, we will explore common time wasters, their detrimental effects, and provide practical strategies for avoiding and minimizing their impact. By eliminating or reducing time-wasting activities, you can make the most of your limited time and focus on what truly matters.

THE IMPACT OF TIME WASTERS

Time wasters are activities or habits that consume a significant amount of time without providing meaningful value or contributing to our goals and priorities. Engaging in time-wasting activities not only squanders valuable minutes but also leads to decreased productivity, increased stress, and missed opportunities. Understanding the impact of time wasters is crucial for reclaiming control over your time and maximizing its potential.

Some common consequences of time wasters include:

Reduced productivity: Engaging in activities that do not contribute to your goals or responsibilities diminishes your productivity. Time wasters divert your attention from important tasks and hinder progress.

Increased stress and overwhelm: Spending excessive time on low-value activities leads to increased stress and a sense of overwhelm. As deadlines approach and important tasks pile up, the pressure intensifies, exacerbating stress levels.

Missed opportunities: Every moment spent on time wasters is a missed opportunity to engage in meaningful activities, learn new skills, or pursue personal growth. Over time, these missed opportunities can hinder your progress and limit your potential.

Decline in focus and concentration: Regularly engaging in time-wasting activities can erode your ability to focus and concentrate. Distractions and interruptions become more enticing, making it challenging to maintain attention on important tasks.

Impaired decision-making: Time wasters drain mental energy and impair decision-making abilities. When your mind is occupied with trivial or unimportant activities, you may struggle to make sound judgments or prioritize effectively.

IDENTIFYING COMMON TIME WASTERS

To effectively avoid time wasters, it is essential to identify and recognize them. Here are some common time-wasting activities to be aware of:

Excessive social media use: Mindlessly scrolling through social media feeds or spending excessive time on platforms like Facebook, Instagram, or Twitter can be a significant time drain.

Internet surfing and browsing: Falling into the rabbit hole of endless internet surfing, reading random articles, or browsing aimlessly without a clear purpose can consume hours of unproductive time.

Procrastination and indecision: Deliberating excessively or putting off important tasks leads to wasted time. Procrastination often results in last-minute rushes and compromised work quality.

Multitasking: Contrary to popular belief, multitasking can hinder productivity and effectiveness. Attempting to do multiple tasks simultaneously leads to divided attention and reduced focus on each task.

Meetings and emails: Unnecessary or unproductive meetings, along with spending excessive time on emails, can consume a significant portion of your workday.

Excessive television or video streaming: Binge-watching television shows or spending hours on video streaming platforms can be a major time sink.

Unproductive conversations: Engaging in lengthy, unproductive conversations that do not contribute to your goals or well-being can waste precious time.

Poor time management: Failing to plan, prioritize, or allocate time effectively can result in scattered efforts and wasted time.

STRATEGIES FOR AVOIDING TIME WASTERS

Avoiding time wasters requires a proactive approach and intentional effort. By implementing the following strategies, you can minimize or eliminate time-wasting activities from your routine:

Set boundaries and time limits: Establish clear boundaries and time limits for activities prone to becoming time wasters. Limit your social media usage to specific time slots or allocate a set amount of time for browsing the internet.

Use website and app blockers: Utilize browser extensions or apps that block or limit access to time-wasting websites or apps during designated work or focused periods.

Practice mindful internet usage: Before accessing the internet, determine your purpose and specific tasks. Stay focused on your objectives and avoid being lured into unrelated or unnecessary browsing.

Implement the Two-Minute Rule: If a task can be completed in two minutes or less, do it immediately rather than postponing it. This prevents small tasks from accumulating and becoming time-consuming later.

Prioritize and plan your day: Use effective time management techniques to prioritize tasks and plan your day in advance. Identify your most important tasks and allocate dedicated time for focused work on them.

Minimize distractions: Create an environment conducive to productivity by minimizing distractions. Put your phone on silent or in another room, close unnecessary tabs on your computer, and create a dedicated workspace that is free from visual distractions.

Practice single-tasking: Focus on one task at a time, dedicating your full attention and effort to it. Single-tasking allows for deeper focus and more efficient completion of tasks.

Delegate or outsource tasks: Identify tasks that can be delegated or outsourced to others. This frees up your time for high-value activities and reduces the burden of low-priority tasks.

Learn to say no: Set boundaries and practice saying no to requests, activities, or commitments that do not align with your priorities. Protecting your time and energy is essential for avoiding time wasters.

Engage in productive breaks: Instead of succumbing to time-wasting activities during breaks, engage in activities that refresh and rejuvenate you. Take a short walk, practice deep breathing exercises, or engage in a brief mindfulness practice.

Foster a productive mindset: Cultivate a mindset that values productivity and recognizes the importance of using time effectively. Develop a sense of purpose and enthusiasm for completing meaningful tasks.

Regularly reassess and adjust: Periodically evaluate your activities and routines to identify any emerging time wasters. Stay vigilant and adapt your strategies as needed to minimize their impact.

OVERCOMING INTERNAL TIME WASTERS

In addition to external time wasters, internal factors can contribute to time wastage. Addressing these internal time wasters is crucial for optimizing your time management. Here are some internal time wasters to be aware of and strategies to overcome them:

Perfectionism and over thinking: Over thinking tasks or seeking perfection can lead to excessive time spent on trivial details. Embrace a growth mindset, focus on progress rather than perfection, and set realistic expectations.

Fear of failure or criticism: Fear can paralyze decision-making and hinder action. Recognize that failure and criticism are part of the learning process and allow yourself to take calculated risks.

Lack of clarity and direction: Vague goals or a lack of clarity can result in aimless actions and wasted effort. Clarify your objectives, break them down into actionable steps, and maintain a clear sense of direction.

Lack of self-discipline: Weak self-discipline can lead to inconsistency and succumbing to distractions. Develop self-discipline through consistent practice, setting routines, and reinforcing positive habits.

Negative mindset and self-doubt: Negative thoughts and self-doubt can undermine your confidence and hinder progress.

Practice self-compassion, challenge negative thinking patterns, and cultivate a positive mindset.

CULTIVATING TIME-CONSCIOUS HABITS

Avoiding time wasters is not a one-time effort but a continuous practice. Cultivate time-conscious habits that support effective time management and minimize time wastage. Here are habits to develop:

Regularly review and reflect on your activities: Periodically assess how you spend your time, identifying any emerging time wasters. Reflect on the impact of your activities on your goals and make necessary adjustments.

Prioritize self-care: Take care of your physical and mental well-being. Prioritize activities such as exercise, adequate sleep, and relaxation to ensure you have the energy and focus necessary to avoid time wasters.

Practice time-blocking and scheduling: Allocate specific time blocks for different tasks and activities using time-blocking techniques. Stick to your schedule, making conscious choices about how you allocate your time.

Develop a morning routine: Establish a morning routine that sets a positive tone for the day. Start your day with activities that energize and prepare you for focused work, such as meditation, exercise, or journaling.

Continuously seek personal growth: Engage in activities that promote personal growth and skill development. Read books, attend workshops, or take online courses that align with your interests and goals.

Regularly reassess your commitments: Periodically evaluate your commitments and activities, ensuring they align with your priorities and goals. Let go of commitments that no longer serve you and create space for more meaningful activities.

Set realistic expectations: Avoid overloading your schedule or setting unrealistic expectations. Be realistic about what you can accomplish within a given timeframe and avoid over committing yourself.

Celebrate achievements: Acknowledge and celebrate your achievements, both big and small. Recognize the progress you have made and reward you for staying focused and avoiding time wasters.

In Conclusion avoiding time wasters is crucial for optimizing your time and increasing your productivity. By identifying common time wasters, implementing effective strategies, and cultivating time-conscious habits, you can minimize the impact of time-wasting activities and make the most of your limited time. In the next chapter, we will explore techniques for enhancing focus and concentration, enabling you to accomplish tasks more efficiently and effectively.

CHAPTER 9: EFFECTIVE PLANNING TECHNIQUES

E ffective planning is essential for maximizing productivity, managing priorities, and making the most of your time. In this chapter, we delve into the importance of planning, explore various planning techniques, and provide practical strategies for implementing effective planning into your daily life. By mastering these techniques, you can optimize your time, stay organized, and achieve your goals with greater efficiency.

THE IMPORTANCE OF PLANNING

Planning plays a pivotal role in time management and goal achievement. It allows you to establish a roadmap for success, set clear objectives, and allocate resources effectively. Here are some key reasons why planning is vital:

Clarity of objectives: Planning provides clarity on what you want to achieve. By defining your goals and objectives, you can prioritize your tasks and align your efforts with what truly matters.

Resource allocation: Effective planning helps you allocate your resources, such as time, energy, and skills, in the most efficient manner. It ensures that you invest your resources wisely, optimizing your productivity and minimizing wastage.

Prioritization: Planning enables you to identify and prioritize tasks based on their importance and urgency. By focusing on high-priority activities, you can make significant progress towards your goals.

Time optimization: With proper planning, you can make the best use of your time. By allocating time slots for specific tasks, setting realistic deadlines, and minimizing time wastage, you can enhance your productivity and accomplish more in less time.

Reduction of stress and overwhelm: Planning helps alleviate stress and overwhelm by breaking down complex tasks into manageable steps. It provides a sense of structure and control, allowing you to approach your work with greater ease and confidence.

EFFECTIVE PLANNING TECHNIQUES

There are various planning techniques and tools available to help you organize your tasks, set goals, and manage your time effectively. Here, we explore some popular techniques and strategies that can enhance your planning process:

Smart goals setting

SMART (Specific, Measurable, Achievable, Relevant, Time-bound) goals is a widely recognized technique for effective planning. SMART goals provide clarity and focus, making them easier to track and achieve. Here's how to create SMART goals:

Specific: Define your goals with precision, ensuring they are clear and specific. Avoid vague or broad statements. Instead, make your goals specific by including details such as what, why, and how.

Measurable: Establish criteria to measure your progress and success. Define specific metrics or milestones that will indicate your progress and allow you to track your achievements.

Achievable: Set goals that are challenging yet attainable. Consider your resources, skills, and limitations to ensure your goals are within reach. Setting overly ambitious goals can lead to frustration and burnout.

Relevant: Ensure that your goals align with your broader objectives and values. Your goals should be relevant and meaningful to you, supporting your long-term vision and purpose.

Time-bound: Assign deadlines to your goals to create a sense of urgency and accountability. Set specific dates or timeframes for completion to maintain focus and momentum.

By incorporating the SMART framework into your planning process, you can create goals that are well-defined, actionable, and motivating.

Prioritization techniques

Effectively prioritizing tasks is a critical aspect of planning. Here are some techniques that can help you prioritize effectively:

Eisenhower Matrix: The Eisenhower Matrix, also known as the Urgent-Important Matrix, categorizes tasks into four quadrants: Urgent and Important, Important but not Urgent, Urgent but not Important, and Neither Urgent nor Important. This matrix helps you identify and prioritize tasks based on their urgency and importance, allowing you to focus on high-priority activities.

ABCDE Method: The ABCDE method, popularized by Brian Tracy, involves assigning priority levels to tasks. Label tasks as A (must-do tasks with significant consequences), B (should-do tasks), C (nice-to-do tasks), D (delegate tasks), and E (eliminate tasks). This method helps you focus on essential tasks while delegating or eliminating non-essential ones.

80/20 Rule: The 80/20 rule, also known as the Pareto Principle, suggests that 80% of your results come from 20% of your efforts. Identify the 20% of tasks that yield the most significant outcomes and prioritize them accordingly.

Choose a prioritization technique that resonates with you and aligns with your working style. Experiment with different methods to find the one that suits you best.

Time blocking

Time blocking involves allocating specific time blocks for different tasks or activities. It helps you create structure and provides a visual representation of how you intend to spend your time. Here's how to implement time blocking effectively:

Start with a weekly overview: Begin by creating a high-level overview of your week. Identify recurring commitments, such as work, meetings, or personal appointments, and allocate dedicated time blocks for them.

Identify your priorities: Determine your most important tasks or goals for the week. Allocate focused time blocks for these activities to ensure they receive the attention they deserve.

Break tasks into smaller blocks: For larger tasks or projects, break them down into smaller, manageable subtasks. Allocate separate time blocks for each subtask to ensure progress.

Consider energy levels and preferences: Take into account your energy levels and preferences when scheduling tasks. Allocate high-energy periods for activities that require focus and concentration.

Protect your time blocks: Once you allocate time blocks for specific tasks, treat them as sacred. Avoid scheduling conflicting appointments or distractions during these periods, and commit to honoring your time commitments.

Time blocking provides structure, eliminates ambiguity, and helps you maintain focus. It is a powerful technique for managing your time effectively and ensuring that important tasks receive the attention they deserve.

To-do lists and task management

To-do lists are simple yet effective tools for managing tasks and maintaining productivity. Here are some tips for creating and managing your to-do lists:

Use a trusted system: Choose a reliable system or tool for managing your to-do lists, such as a digital task management app, a physical planner, or a simple notebook. Find a system that suits your preferences and allows for easy organization and tracking.

Break tasks into actionable steps: Instead of listing vague tasks, break them down into specific, actionable steps. This provides clarity and makes tasks more manageable.

Prioritize tasks: Assign priorities to your tasks to ensure you tackle the most important ones first. Use techniques like the Eisenhower Matrix or the ABCDE method to prioritize effectively.

Set realistic expectations: Be realistic about what you can accomplish within a given timeframe. Avoid overloading your to-do list, as this can lead to overwhelm and decreased productivity.

Regularly review and update: Review and update your to-do list regularly. Check off completed tasks, reassess priorities, and add or remove tasks as needed.

By implementing effective task management techniques, you can stay organized, track your progress, and ensure that important tasks are completed on time.

STRATEGIES FOR EFFECTIVE PLANNING

In addition to specific planning techniques, incorporating the following strategies into your planning process will enhance its effectiveness:

Establish clear objectives

Before you begin planning, establish clear objectives. Clearly define what you want to achieve and why it is important to you. Clarity of objectives provides a sense of purpose and helps you align your planning efforts with your long-term goals.

Break down tasks

Break down complex tasks or projects into smaller, manageable steps. This enables you to approach your work systematically, reducing overwhelm and making tasks more achievable. Breaking down tasks also allows for better estimation of time and resources required.

Consider Deadlines and Time Constraints

When planning, consider deadlines and time constraints associated with your tasks. Be realistic about the time required to complete each task and ensure that your overall schedule aligns with your commitments and deadlines.

Anticipate and Plan for Contingencies

Account for unexpected events or setbacks by planning for contingencies. Leave buffer time in your schedule to accommodate unforeseen circumstances or emergencies. This flexibility allows you to adapt to changes without derailing your entire plan.

Regularly Review and Adjust

Regularly review your plans and progress to ensure they remain relevant and effective. Assess whether you are on track to achieve your goals, identify any bottlenecks or obstacles, and make necessary adjustments to your plan.

Practice Time Management Techniques

Incorporate effective time management techniques into your planning process. Techniques such as time blocking, Pomodoro Technique (working in focused intervals with timed breaks), and batch processing (grouping similar tasks together) can enhance your productivity and efficiency.

Maintain Flexibility

While planning is essential, it is equally important to remain flexible. Be open to adapting your plans as circumstances change or new opportunities arise. Flexibility allows for spontaneity and ensures that your plans remain aligned with your evolving needs and priorities.

IMPLEMENTING EFFECTIVE PLANNING INTO DAILY LIFE

To effectively implement planning techniques into your daily life, consider the following strategies:

Make planning a habit: Dedicate regular time for planning, whether it's at the start or end of each day, or on a weekly basis. Consistency is key to developing the habit of planning and making it an integral part of your routine.

Use technology to your advantage: Leverage digital tools, apps, or software that can streamline your planning process and make it more convenient. Explore productivity apps, calendar tools, or project management software that align with your needs and preferences.

Find what works for you: Experiment with different planning techniques, tools, and approaches to find what works best for you. Everyone has unique preferences and working styles, so customize your planning process to suit your individual needs.

Reflect and learn from experience: Regularly reflect on your planning efforts and learn from your experiences. Assess what worked well and what could be improved. Continuously refine your planning process based on these insights.

Seek support and accountability: Engage with accountability partners, mentors, or colleagues who can provide support, guidance, and feedback. Sharing your plans and progress with others fosters accountability and motivates you to stay on track.

9.5 Long-Term Planning and Goal Setting Effective planning extends beyond daily or short-term activities. Long-term planning and goal setting are vital for creating a roadmap to success. Here are some strategies for long-term planning:

Define your vision: Clarify your long-term vision and desired outcomes. Understand where you want to be in the future and set goals that align with your vision.

Break down long-term goals: Break down your long-term goals into shorter-term milestones or objectives. This allows you to track progress, make adjustments, and maintain momentum towards your ultimate vision.

Create a timeline: Establish a timeline for achieving your long-term goals. Identify key milestones and set specific deadlines for each stage of your plan.

Review and adjust periodically: Regularly review and reassess your long-term plan. As circumstances change, adjust your goals and strategies accordingly to ensure they remain relevant and achievable.

Stay focused and motivated: Maintain focus on your long-term goals by regularly reminding yourself of their importance and relevance. Stay motivated by celebrating milestones and recognizing the progress you have made.

By incorporating long-term planning into your overall planning process, you create a clear path towards your desired outcomes and increase the likelihood of achieving your vision.

DEALING WITH UNEXPECTED CHANGES

Even with effective planning, unexpected changes or disruptions can occur. Here are strategies for dealing with unforeseen circumstances:

Maintain adaptability: Cultivate an adaptable mindset that allows you to respond to changes and adjust your plans as needed. Embrace flexibility and view unexpected changes as opportunities for growth and adaptation.

Prioritize and reprioritize: When faced with unexpected changes reassess your priorities and reprioritize tasks accordingly. Determine what is most important in light of the new circumstances and adjust your plan accordingly.

Seek support and guidance: Reach out to mentors, colleagues, or support networks for guidance and advice when unexpected changes arise. Others may offer valuable insights or alternative perspectives to help you navigate through challenging times.

Learn from the experience: Reflect on the unexpected changes and learn from the experience. Assess how you handled the situation, identify any areas for improvement, and integrate the lessons learned into your future planning efforts.

IMPLEMENTING PLANNING FOR WORK-LIFE BALANCE

Effective planning is not limited to professional tasks alone but extends to all aspects of your life. By incorporating planning techniques into your personal life, you can achieve a better work-life balance. Here are some strategies:

Allocate time for personal priorities: Schedule time for activities that are important to you, such as self-care, hobbies, family time, or socializing. Treat personal commitments with the same level of importance as professional ones.

Set boundaries: Establish clear boundaries between work and personal life. Avoid letting work spill over into personal time by setting dedicated hours for work and creating a separation between your professional and personal spaces.

Prioritize self-care: Make self-care a priority by allocating time for activities that recharge and rejuvenate you. This could include exercise, meditation, hobbies, or spending time in nature.

Regularly assess and adjust: Continuously assess how your planning efforts impact your work-life balance. Regularly evaluate your commitments, adjust priorities, and make necessary changes to ensure you maintain a healthy equilibrium.

In Conclusion Effective planning is the cornerstone of efficient time management and goal achievement. By implementing planning techniques, setting SMART goals, and prioritizing tasks, you can optimize your productivity, reduce stress, and make the most of your limited time. In the next chapter, we will explore strategies for effective decision-making, enabling you to make informed choices and use your time wisely.

CHAPTER 10: DELEGATION AND OUTSOURCING

Delegation and outsourcing are powerful strategies for maximizing your time, enhancing productivity, and focusing on high-value tasks. In this chapter, we will explore the benefits of delegation and outsourcing, provide practical tips for effective implementation, and discuss how these strategies can help you make the most of your limited time.

THE POWER OF DELEGATION

Delegation involves entrusting tasks and responsibilities to others, allowing you to leverage their skills and expertise while freeing up your time for more important activities. Here are some key benefits of delegation:

Time optimization: Delegation enables you to delegate routine or less important tasks to others, freeing up your time to focus on high-value activities that require your unique skills and expertise.

Enhanced productivity: By delegating tasks to capable individuals, you can distribute the workload more efficiently and accomplish more in less time. Delegation allows you to leverage the strengths of others and tap into their expertise, resulting in improved productivity.

Skill development: Delegating tasks provides an opportunity for team members or colleagues to develop new skills and grow professionally. Delegation fosters a sense of trust and empowerment, empowering individuals to take on new challenges and expand their capabilities.

Improved collaboration: Delegation encourages collaboration and teamwork within an organization. By distributing tasks among team members, you promote a sense of shared responsibility and foster a collaborative work environment.

Focus on strategic activities: Delegation allows you to shift your focus from operational or administrative tasks to strategic activities that drive growth and innovation. By delegating routine tasks, you can dedicate more time and energy to critical decision-making and long-term planning.

EFFECTIVE DELEGATION STRATEGIES

To effectively delegate tasks, consider the following strategies:

Assess task suitability

When delegating tasks, consider their nature and complexity. Some tasks are more suitable for delegation than others. Factors to consider include:

Repetitive or routine tasks: Tasks that are repetitive or routine in nature are prime candidates for delegation. These tasks can often be easily taught and do not require your specific expertise.

Skill requirements: Assess the skill level required for the task. Delegate tasks that align with the skills and capabilities of the individual or team members you are delegating to.

Time constraints: Consider whether the task can be completed within a reasonable timeframe by someone else. Delegating tasks with tight deadlines may not be feasible if there is insufficient time to train or familiarize others with the task.

Select the right individuals

When delegating tasks, it is essential to select the right individuals or team members. Consider the following factors:

Competence and capabilities: Identify individuals who have the necessary skills, knowledge, and experience to handle the delegated tasks effectively.

Interest and motivation: Choose individuals who demonstrate an interest in the task or a willingness to learn. Motivated individuals are more likely to take ownership of the task and deliver high-quality results.

Workload and availability: Assess the workload and availability of potential delegates to ensure they have the capacity to take on additional responsibilities without becoming overwhelmed.

Training and support: Provide appropriate training and support to individuals who may need to acquire new skills or knowledge to perform the delegated tasks effectively. Offer guidance and resources to ensure their success.

Clearly communicate expectations

Clear and concise communication is vital when delegating tasks. Ensure that the delegated individual or team understands the following:

Task objectives: Clearly articulate the objectives, expected outcomes, and deliverables associated with the task. Provide sufficient context to help them understand the purpose and importance of their role in achieving the desired results.

Scope and boundaries: Define the boundaries of the delegated task, including any constraints, limitations, or guidelines that need to be followed. Communicate the expected level of autonomy and decision-making authority.

Deadlines and milestones: Set clear deadlines and milestones to ensure timely completion of the task. Establish a mechanism for regular progress updates and check-ins to track progress and address any challenges.

Performance standards: Clearly communicate the expected standards of quality and performance for the delegated task. Provide guidelines, benchmarks, or examples to clarify expectations.

Provide ongoing support and feedback

Support and feedback are crucial elements of effective delegation. Provide the following support throughout the delegated task:

Guidance and resources: Offer guidance, resources, and necessary tools to facilitate the successful completion of the task. Ensure that individuals have access to the information and materials they need to perform their role effectively.

Regular check-ins: Schedule regular check-ins to assess progress, offer assistance, and address any questions or concerns. These check-ins demonstrate your commitment to their success and provide an opportunity for course correction if needed.

Encourage questions and open communication: Create an environment that encourages individuals to ask questions, seek clarification, and share their insights. Open communication fosters collaboration and ensures that everyone is aligned.

Constructive feedback: Provide timely and constructive feedback on the performance of delegated tasks. Recognize and acknowledge successes, offer guidance for improvement, and provide constructive criticism when necessary.

Trust and empower

Delegation is based on trust and empowerment. Trust the individuals you delegate tasks to, and empower them to take ownership and make decisions. Trusting your team members fosters a sense of responsibility and accountability, and it encourages them to perform at their best.

THE POWER OF OUTSOURCING

Outsourcing involves delegating specific tasks or projects to external individuals or organizations. Here are some key benefits of outsourcing:

Access to specialized expertise: Outsourcing allows you to tap into the expertise and skills of professionals or specialized service providers who have the knowledge and experience in a specific domain. This enables you to benefit from their expertise without having to develop it in-house.

Cost-effectiveness: Outsourcing can be a cost-effective solution, particularly for tasks or projects that require specialized knowledge or resources. Instead of investing in hiring, training, or acquiring tools, you can leverage external resources at a fraction of the cost.

Time savings: By outsourcing tasks, you can save valuable time and redirect your focus on core activities that require your attention. Outsourcing time-consuming or repetitive tasks enables you to streamline your workflow and increase overall productivity.

Scalability and flexibility: Outsourcing offers flexibility in scaling your operations. You can easily adjust the level of outsourcing based on your needs, without the constraints of hiring and managing additional staff.

Increased efficiency: By outsourcing non-core activities, you can streamline your business processes and enhance efficiency. This allows you to allocate your resources more effectively and concentrate on activities that directly contribute to your strategic objectives.

EFFECTIVE OUTSOURCING STRATEGIES

When considering outsourcing, keep the following strategies in mind:

Identify suitable tasks for outsourcing

Not all tasks are suitable for outsourcing. Consider the following factors when identifying tasks for outsourcing:

Specialized knowledge or expertise: Tasks that require specialized knowledge or expertise outside your organization's core capabilities are ideal candidates for outsourcing. These tasks may include graphic design, website development, copywriting, or accounting services.

Time-consuming activities: Outsource tasks that are time-consuming but not directly related to your core activities. This allows you to free up your time for high-value tasks that require your unique skills and expertise.

Cost-benefit analysis: Conduct a cost-benefit analysis to determine whether outsourcing a particular task is more cost-effective than performing it in-house. Consider factors such as labor costs, training expenses, and equipment investments.

Research and select reliable outsourcing partners

When outsourcing, research and select reliable outsourcing partners or service providers. Consider the following criteria:

Expertise and experience: Look for providers who have a track record of delivering high-quality results and have experience in the specific task or domain you are outsourcing.

Reputation and references: Seek recommendations or references from trusted sources to ensure the reliability and credibility of potential outsourcing partners. Research online reviews, testimonials, or case studies to gain insights into their performance.

Clear communication: Choose partners who communicate effectively, respond promptly to inquiries, and understand your specific requirements. Clear and open communication is crucial for successful outsourcing partnerships.

Confidentiality and security: Assess the provider's commitment to confidentiality and data security. Ensure that appropriate measures are in place to protect your sensitive information.

Clearly define expectations and deliverables

Clearly define your expectations and deliverables when outsourcing tasks. Provide the following details to outsourcing partners:

Task requirements: Clearly articulate your requirements, objectives, and specifications to ensure that the outsourcing partner understands your expectations.

Quality standards: Communicate your expectations regarding quality standards, including benchmarks or specific criteria that need to be met.

Timelines and milestones: Establish clear timelines and milestones for the task. This allows you to track progress and ensure that the project remains on schedule.

Regular communication channels: Determine the mode and frequency of communication with the outsourcing partner. Establish regular check-ins to address any questions or concerns and maintain open lines of communication.

Establish a contract or agreement

When outsourcing tasks, establish a contract or agreement that outlines the terms and conditions of the partnership. Key elements to include in the contract are:

Scope of work: Clearly define the scope of work, including specific tasks, responsibilities, and deliverables.

Timelines and milestones: Outline the agreed-upon timelines and milestones for the project.

Payment terms: Specify the payment terms, including rates, invoicing schedules, and any additional fees or expenses.

Confidentiality and data protection: Include provisions regarding the protection of confidential information and data security.

Termination clauses: Define the conditions under which either party can terminate the agreement and specify any notice periods required.

Maintain effective communication and feedback

Maintain open communication channels with outsourcing partners and provide feedback throughout the project. Regularly assess progress, provide constructive feedback, and address any concerns promptly. This ensures that the project remains on track and allows for adjustments if necessary.

Finding the Balance: Delegation vs. Outsourcing

Determining whether to delegate tasks internally or outsource them externally requires careful consideration. Here are some factors to help you find the right balance:

Core competencies: Tasks that are core to your organization's competencies or unique value proposition are best kept in-house. These tasks define your expertise and differentiate you from competitors.

Cost-effectiveness: Evaluate the cost-effectiveness of performing a task in-house versus outsourcing it. Consider factors such as labor costs, training expenses, equipment investments, and the potential impact on productivity.

Expertise and resources: Assess whether your internal team has the necessary expertise, capacity, and resources to handle the task effectively. If not, outsourcing may be a viable option to tap into specialized knowledge or resources.

Time constraints: Evaluate the urgency and time constraints associated with the task. If your team lacks the bandwidth to handle the task within the required timeframe, outsourcing can provide a timely solution.

Strategic focus: Consider how the task aligns with your strategic objectives and core priorities. Tasks that directly contribute to your strategic goals may be best handled internally, while non-core activities can be outsourced to free up your time and resources.

Overcoming Challenges and Ensuring Success

Delegation and outsourcing can present challenges that need to be addressed to ensure success. Here are some common challenges and strategies for overcoming them:

Communication gaps: Ensure clear and open lines of communication between you and those to whom you delegate or outsource tasks. Establish regular check-ins, provide clear instructions, and encourage feedback to bridge any communication gaps.

Trust and control: Overcoming the need for complete control is crucial when delegating or outsourcing tasks. Build trust in your team members or outsourcing partners by providing clear expectations, supporting their efforts, and focusing on outcomes rather than micromanagement.

Training and guidance: When delegating tasks, provide appropriate training and support to ensure that individuals have the necessary skills and knowledge to perform their roles effectively. When outsourcing, communicate requirements clearly and provide necessary guidelines and resources.

Quality control: Implement mechanisms to ensure quality control for delegated tasks or outsourced projects. Establish quality standards, provide feedback, and perform regular reviews to ensure that the desired outcomes are met.

Transition and handover: When transitioning tasks to others, ensure a smooth handover by providing comprehensive documentation, clear instructions, and sufficient time for knowledge transfer. This helps prevent disruptions and ensures a seamless transition.

MAINTAINING A GROWTH MINDSET

To make the most of delegation and outsourcing, adopt a

growth mindset. Embrace the opportunities these strategies provide for growth and development. Be open to learning from others, embracing new ideas, and continuously improving your delegation and outsourcing practices.

By effectively delegating tasks and outsourcing non-core activities, you can leverage the skills and expertise of others, optimize your time, and focus on activities that drive growth and value. In the next chapter, we will explore strategies for managing distractions and maintaining focus, enabling you to make the most of your time in an increasingly distracting world.

CHAPTER 11:
SAYING NO

In a world filled with endless opportunities and demands, learning to say no is a crucial skill for valuing your time and protecting your priorities. In this chapter, we will explore the power of saying no, the reasons why it can be challenging, and practical strategies for effectively saying no without guilt or resentment. By mastering the art of saying no, you can reclaim control over your time, focus on what truly matters, and live a more intentional and fulfilling life.

THE POWER OF SAYING NO

Saying no is often seen as a negative or difficult act. However, it is an essential tool for effective time management and maintaining a healthy work-life balance. Here are some key reasons why saying no is powerful:

Protecting your priorities: Saying no allows you to protect your priorities and focus on what matters most to you. By setting boundaries and declining commitments that do not align with your values or goals, you create space for activities that truly contribute to your personal and professional growth.

Managing your time and energy: When you say no to requests or tasks that are not essential or aligned with your objectives, you conserve your time and energy for activities that have a higher impact and bring you closer to your goals. Saying no helps prevent overwhelm and burnout by ensuring you have the capacity to tackle what truly matters.

Honoring your values: By saying no, you can stay true to your values and principles. It allows you to make choices that align with your beliefs and avoid compromising your integrity by taking on commitments that go against your core values.

Creating boundaries: Saying no establishes clear boundaries in your personal and professional life. It communicates your limits, setting expectations with others about what you are willing and able to take on. Boundaries are essential for maintaining healthy relationships, avoiding over commitment, and avoiding unnecessary stress.

Enhancing productivity and effectiveness: By saying no to non-essential tasks or distractions, you can focus your time and attention on activities that have the most significant impact. This enhances your productivity and effectiveness, allowing you to achieve better results in less time.

THE CHALLENGES OF SAYING NO

Despite its benefits, saying no can be challenging for many individuals. Here are some common reasons why saying no can be difficult:

Fear of missing out (FOMO): The fear of missing out on opportunities or disappointing others can make it challenging to say no. You may worry about the potential consequences of declining an invitation or request, such as being left out or damaging relationships.

Desire to please others: Many people have a natural inclination to please others and fear rejection or disapproval. The desire to be liked or accepted can make it difficult to say no, as it may be perceived as a rejection or disappointment to the person making the request.

Lack of assertiveness: Assertiveness is a crucial skill

for effectively saying no. Individuals who struggle with assertiveness may find it challenging to express their needs and set boundaries, leading to difficulty in saying no.

Guilt and obligation: Feelings of guilt or obligation can arise when saying no. You may feel guilty for not being able to accommodate every request or obligated to say yes due to societal or personal expectations.

Uncertainty and indecision: Sometimes, the inability to say no stems from uncertainty or indecision. You may be unsure about your priorities or feel hesitant about declining an opportunity without fully understanding its potential impact.

STRATEGIES FOR EFFECTIVE SAYING NO

Mastering the art of saying no requires practice and the implementation of effective strategies. Here are practical tips to help you say no confidently and respectfully:

Clarify your priorities

Before responding to requests, take time to clarify your priorities. Understand what truly matters to you and align your decisions with your values and goals. This clarity empowers you to make deliberate choices and confidently say no to opportunities or tasks that do not align with your priorities.

Practice self-awareness

Develop self-awareness to recognize your limits, capacity, and personal boundaries. Understand your strengths, weaknesses, and the level of commitment you can comfortably handle. Being aware of your own needs and limitations enables you to say no more effectively without overextending yourself.

Use the pause and reflect technique

When faced with a request, give yourself time to pause and reflect before responding. Avoid the urge to provide an immediate answer. Take a moment to evaluate the request and assess its alignment with your priorities. This pause allows you to respond thoughtfully and make an informed decision.

Be polite and respectful

When saying no, it is essential to be polite and respectful. Express gratitude for the opportunity or invitation and acknowledge the person's request. Clearly communicate your reasons for declining and provide a brief explanation if necessary. By showing respect and kindness in your response, you maintain positive relationships while still asserting your boundaries.

Offer alternatives or compromises

If appropriate, offer alternatives or compromises when saying no. Suggest alternative solutions, resources, or individuals who may be better suited to fulfill the request. This demonstrates your willingness to help within your capacity and can soften the impact of your decline.

Be assertive and firm

Assertiveness is key when saying no. Be firm and clear in your response, avoiding vague or ambiguous language. Use assertive statements such as "I appreciate the offer, but I am unable to take it on at this time" or "I have to decline as it does not align with my current priorities." Assertiveness reinforces your boundaries and sends a clear message.

Practice saying no

Like any skill, saying no improves with practice. Start with smaller requests or situations where the stakes are lower. Gradually build your confidence and assertiveness in saying no. As you gain experience and witness the positive outcomes of saying no, it becomes easier to decline more significant commitments.

Set and communicate boundaries

Establish clear boundaries for yourself and communicate them effectively. Let others know your limitations and preferred ways of working. Setting boundaries upfront reduces the likelihood of receiving requests that do not align with your capacity or priorities.

Develop a standard response

Prepare a standard response or script that you can use when saying no. Having a rehearsed response helps you respond confidently and consistently, even in unexpected situations. Modify the script as needed to fit the specific context while maintaining your core message.

Seek support and accountability

If saying no is particularly challenging for you, seek support and accountability from trusted friends, colleagues, or mentors. Discuss your struggles and goals with them, and ask for their guidance and encouragement. Having someone to support you throughout the process can boost your confidence and provide valuable insights.

EMBRACING THE POSITIVE EFFECTS OF SAYING NO

Saying no not only benefits you but also creates positive effects in various aspects of your life. Here are some positive outcomes of effectively saying no:

Improved time management: Saying no helps you prioritize your time and allocate it to activities that align with your goals. This improves your time management skills, increases your productivity, and reduces overwhelm.

Enhanced self-care: By saying no to commitments that drain your energy or compromise your well-being, you create space for self-care. Prioritizing your needs and self-care activities improves your overall physical and mental health.

Strengthened relationships: Respectful and honest communication when saying no fosters stronger and healthier relationships. People appreciate your honesty and value your ability to set boundaries. Saying no can lead to deeper connections based on mutual respect and understanding.

Increased focus and productivity: By saying no to distractions or tasks that do not align with your priorities, you can maintain focus on essential activities. This enhances your productivity, allowing you to achieve better results in less time.

Greater self-confidence: Successfully saying no builds your self-confidence and assertiveness. As you assert your boundaries and make decisions aligned with your values, you develop a stronger sense of self and build resilience.

Opportunities for growth: Saying no to certain opportunities creates space for new and more meaningful ones. It opens doors to experiences, projects, and relationships that align with your goals and values, facilitating personal and professional growth.

OVERCOMING GUILT AND HANDLING REACTIONS

Despite the positive effects of saying no, guilt may still arise when declining requests. Here are strategies to overcome guilt and handle reactions:

Understand your guilt

Recognize that guilt is a natural response when saying no, but it does not diminish the validity of your decision. Understand that it is normal to prioritize your needs and well-being, and saying no is not a selfish act.

Reframe your perspective

Reframe your perspective by focusing on the positive aspects of saying no. Remind yourself of the benefits, such as maintaining balance, honoring your priorities, and creating opportunities for others to step up or collaborate.

Communicate with empathy

When handling reactions to your no, respond with empathy and understanding. Acknowledge the other person's feelings, but remain firm in your decision. Help them understand that your decision is not a personal rejection but a result of your priorities and limitations.

Stay resilient

Expect some resistance or disappointment from others when you say no. Stay resilient and confident in your decision. Remind yourself of your priorities and the value of your time. Over time, handling reactions becomes easier as you become more comfortable with asserting your boundaries.

SAYING NO IN DIFFERENT AREAS OF LIFE

The skill of saying no applies to various areas of life, including personal, professional, and social contexts. Here are examples of how saying no can be applied in different areas:

Professional context

Declining additional work assignments that exceed your capacity or fall outside your scope of responsibility.

Saying no to meetings or events that are not directly relevant to your objectives or do not contribute to your professional growth.

Politely declining requests for help or collaboration that are not aligned with your expertise or availability.

Personal context

Saying no to social invitations or events that do not align with your personal interests, values, or energy levels.

Declining requests for volunteering or joining committees when your plate is already full.

Setting boundaries with family or friends regarding your time and availability, ensuring you have adequate personal time and space.

Social context

Politely declining invitations or requests to join groups, clubs, or committees that do not align with your interests or priorities.

Saying no to requests for favors or activities that stretch your resources or time without reciprocal benefits.

Setting limits on social commitments to ensure you have time for self-care and relaxation.

SAYING NO TO YOURSELF

Saying no to yourself is just as important as saying no to others. It involves setting boundaries and making conscious choices that align with your goals and well-being. Here are some areas where saying no to yourself can be beneficial:

Saying no to distractions or time-wasting activities that hinder your productivity and progress.

Declining impulsive purchases or unnecessary expenditures that derail your financial goals.

Setting boundaries on work hours and saying no to the temptation to overwork or neglect self-care.

Saying no to negative self-talk, self-doubt, or limiting beliefs that hinder your personal growth and success.

Prioritizing your well-being by saying no to excessive demands or expectations, allowing yourself to rest and recharge.

EMBRACING THE FREEDOM OF SAYING NO

Saying no is not a negative act, but rather an empowering choice that enables you to prioritize your time, energy, and values. Embrace the freedom that comes with saying no, and recognize it as a tool for self-care, growth, and intentional living.

By effectively saying no, you create space for what truly matters, cultivate healthier relationships, and maintain balance in all areas of your life. In the next chapter, we will explore the concept of self-reflection and its role in valuing your time and making intentional choices.

CHAPTER 12: TIME BLOCKING TECHNIQUES

Time is a finite resource, and managing it effectively is crucial for personal and professional success. One powerful technique for optimizing your time is time blocking. In this chapter, we will delve into the concept of time blocking, explore its benefits, and provide practical strategies for implementing various time blocking techniques. By mastering time blocking, you can enhance productivity, reduce distractions, and make the most of your limited time.

UNDERSTANDING TIME BLOCKING

Time blocking is a time management technique that involves dividing your day into distinct blocks of time dedicated to specific tasks or activities. By allocating specific time periods for different tasks, you create a structured schedule that helps you stay focused, organized, and efficient.

The fundamental principle of time blocking is that you proactively plan and allocate time for each task or activity, rather than simply reacting to incoming requests or working on tasks as they arise. By doing so, you take control of your schedule and prioritize your most important activities, ensuring that they receive the attention they deserve.

THE BENEFITS OF TIME BLOCKING

Time blocking offers a range of benefits that can significantly enhance your productivity and time management skills. Here are some key advantages of implementing time blocking techniques:

Enhanced focus and concentration: Time blocking provides structure and eliminates ambiguity in your schedule. By dedicating specific blocks of time to each task, you can fully immerse yourself in the activity without distractions, leading to improved focus and concentration.

Improved productivity: Time blocking enables you to prioritize tasks and allocate time based on their importance and urgency. This ensures that you allocate sufficient time and attention to high-priority activities, resulting in increased productivity and accomplishment of critical tasks.

Effective task management: By assigning dedicated blocks of time to different tasks or projects, you can better manage your workload. Time blocking allows you to visualize the time required for each task, ensuring that you allocate adequate time and avoid over commitment.

Reduction of multitasking: Multitasking can be detrimental to productivity and focus. Time blocking promotes single-tasking by allocating specific time slots for each activity. This encourages you to focus on one task at a time, leading to improved efficiency and quality of work.

Enhanced time awareness: Time blocking increases your awareness of how you spend your time. By visualizing your schedule and the time allocated to each task, you gain a better understanding of where your time is being invested and can identify areas for improvement or adjustment.

Effective goal management: Time blocking helps align your tasks and activities with your goals. By dedicating specific time blocks to activities that contribute to your objectives, you ensure progress towards your goals and reduce the risk of neglecting important areas of your life or work.

Reduced stress and overwhelm: Time blocking reduces stress and overwhelm by providing a clear structure and plan for your day. When you know exactly what tasks you need to complete and when, you experience a sense of control and are less likely to feel overwhelmed by competing demands.

IMPLEMENTING TIME BLOCKING TECHNIQUES

To effectively implement time blocking techniques, consider the following strategies:

Identify and Prioritize Tasks

Start by identifying your tasks and activities. Make a list of all the tasks you need to accomplish, both professional and personal. Categorize them based on their priority and urgency. Identify tasks that require focused attention and allocate more time to them in your schedule.

Determine Time Blocks

Once you have identified your tasks, allocate specific time blocks for each activity. Consider the nature of the task, its estimated duration, and your energy levels throughout the day. Assign longer time blocks for complex or time-consuming tasks and shorter time blocks for smaller or less demanding activities.

Consider Energy Levels and Peak Performance

Take into account your natural energy levels and peak performance times when scheduling tasks. Allocate high-energy periods for tasks that require intense focus or creativity. Reserve low-energy periods for more routine or administrative tasks that do not demand as much mental or physical energy.

Avoid Over-commitment

Be realistic when allocating time for tasks. Avoid over-commitment by accurately estimating the time required for each activity. Allow buffer time between tasks to account for unforeseen circumstances or transitions. By avoiding over-commitment, you can maintain a sense of balance and avoid feeling rushed or overwhelmed.

Batch Similar Tasks

Consider grouping similar tasks together and scheduling them in consecutive time blocks. This technique, known as task batching, allows you to minimize context switching and optimize your efficiency. For example, allocate a block of time for responding to emails, another for conducting meetings, and another for focused work on specific projects.

Include Breaks and Transition Time

Incorporate regular breaks and transition time between tasks or activities. Breaks help refresh your mind, prevent burnout, and maintain focus. Schedule short breaks between time blocks to stretch, hydrate, or engage in brief relaxation exercises. Also, allow some transition time to mentally switch gears and prepare for the next task.

Be Flexible and Adaptable

While time blocking provides structure, it is essential to remain flexible and adaptable. Unexpected events or new priorities may arise, requiring adjustments to your schedule. Embrace the flexibility to rearrange time blocks as needed while keeping your goals and priorities in mind.

Leverage Technology and Tools

Utilize technology and time management tools to implement time blocking effectively. Digital calendars, productivity apps, or project management software can help you visualize and manage your time blocks more efficiently. These tools can also provide reminders and notifications to keep you on track.

Communicate and Protect Your Time

Communicate your time blocking schedule with colleagues, team members, or family members to ensure they are aware of your availability and commitments. Set boundaries and protect your time blocks from interruptions and distractions. Communicate your need for uninterrupted focus during specific time periods and encourage others to respect your boundaries.

Evaluate and Refine

Regularly evaluate and refine your time blocking approach. Assess the effectiveness of your time blocks, identify areas for improvement, and make adjustments accordingly. Experiment with different techniques, durations, or time allocations to find what works best for you.

ADVANCED TIME BLOCKING TECHNIQUES

In addition to the basic time blocking strategies, there are advanced techniques that can further enhance your time management skills. Here are a few examples:

Theme-Based Time Blocking

Theme-based time blocking involves dedicating specific days or time blocks to specific themes or types of activities. For example, you can allocate Mondays for strategic planning, Tuesdays for client meetings, Wednesdays for focused work, and so on. This approach allows for deep immersion in specific areas and promotes a more balanced workload.

Time Blocking with Priorities

When time blocking, prioritize your tasks based on their importance and align them with your overarching goals or objectives. Allocate time blocks specifically for high-priority activities that have a significant impact on your goals. By giving priority to these tasks, you ensure they receive adequate attention and are not overshadowed by less critical activities.

Time Blocking for Self-Care

It is essential to allocate time blocks for self-care activities. Prioritize your well-being by scheduling time for exercise, relaxation, hobbies, or quality time with loved ones. By dedicating specific time blocks to self-care, you prioritize your physical and mental health, ensuring you have the energy and resilience to tackle other tasks effectively.

Time Blocking for Learning and Growth

Allocate dedicated time blocks for learning and personal growth. Set aside time for reading, attending webinars or workshops, or acquiring new skills. By intentionally scheduling time for learning, you invest in your personal and professional development, expanding your knowledge and staying ahead in your field.

OVERCOMING CHALLENGES AND MAXIMIZING RESULTS

Implementing time blocking techniques may present challenges, but with persistence and adaptation, you can overcome them. Here are strategies to help you maximize the results of your time blocking efforts:

Overcome Resistance to Structure

If you are resistant to structure or prefer a more flexible approach, start gradually by implementing time blocking for specific tasks or periods of the day. Experiment with different levels of structure and observe the impact on your productivity and focus. Over time, you may find that the structure of time blocking actually enhances your creativity and freedom.

Manage Interruptions and Distractions

Interruptions and distractions can disrupt your time blocks and derail your productivity. Minimize interruptions by communicating your availability to colleagues or family members. Utilize techniques such as time-boxing your distractions or implementing focused work practices, like the **Pomodoro** Technique, to minimize the impact of interruptions.

Learn to Adapt and Flexibility

Flexibility is crucial when implementing time blocking techniques. Unexpected events or shifting priorities may require adjustments to your schedule. Embrace adaptability and learn to reallocate time blocks as needed. Avoid rigid adherence to your plan and be open to changes that align with your goals and values.

Build Consistency and Discipline

Consistency and discipline are keys to making time blocking a habit. Commit to your scheduled time blocks and strive to follow them consistently. Over time, the discipline of sticking to your schedule becomes easier, and the benefits of improved productivity and time management become more apparent.

Reflect and Learn from Experience

Regularly reflect on your time blocking experience and learn from it. Evaluate your productivity, focus, and satisfaction with your time allocation. Identify patterns, adjustments, or improvements you can make based on your observations. Continual reflection and learning allow you to refine your time blocking approach and make it increasingly effective.

EMBRACING TIME BLOCKING AS A LIFESTYLE

Time blocking is not merely a technique; it is a mindset and a way of life. Embrace time blocking as a lifestyle by integrating it into your daily routine and decision-making processes. Make conscious choices about how you allocate your time, ensuring that it aligns with your goals and values. Regularly review and adjust your time blocks to reflect changing priorities and objectives.

By fully embracing time blocking as a lifestyle, you can cultivate a sense of control over your time, maximize productivity, and live a more intentional and fulfilling life. In the next chapter, we will explore strategies for overcoming procrastination and improving self-discipline, enabling you to make consistent progress towards your goals.

CHAPTER 13: MANAGING DISTRACTIONS

I n today's fast-paced and technology-driven world, distractions are abundant; making it challenging to stay focused and makes the most of our limited time. In this chapter, we will explore the detrimental effects of distractions, the underlying causes, and practical strategies for effectively managing and minimizing distractions. By mastering the art of managing distractions, you can reclaim control over your time, boost productivity, and achieve your goals with greater ease.

THE IMPACT OF DISTRACTIONS

Distractions can significantly hinder our productivity, focus, and overall well-being. Here are some of the ways distractions can impact our lives:

Reduced productivity: Distractions pull our attention away from the task at hand, resulting in decreased productivity and efficiency. They disrupt our flow and make it difficult to concentrate, leading to longer completion times and lower quality work.

Increased errors: When our attention is divided between multiple tasks or interruptions, we are more prone to making mistakes. Distractions can cause us to overlook important details, leading to errors or oversights that may have negative consequences.

Impaired decision-making: Distractions disrupt our ability to think critically and make informed decisions. They divert our attention from relevant information and impair our judgment, potentially leading to suboptimal choices or missed opportunities.

Elevated stress levels: Constant distractions can lead to increased stress and feelings of overwhelm. The continuous interruptions and the pressure to stay on top of multiple tasks create a sense of urgency and can negatively impact our mental and emotional well-being.

Reduced creativity: Distractions prevent us from entering a state of deep focus necessary for creativity and innovation. They inhibit our ability to think deeply and make connections, hindering our creative problem-solving abilities.

Impacted work-life balance: Distractions can spill over into our personal lives, making it challenging to switch off from work or enjoy quality time with loved ones. The inability to establish boundaries and separate work and personal life can lead to burnout and strained relationships.

UNDERSTANDING THE CAUSES OF DISTRACTIONS

To effectively manage distractions, it is essential to understand their underlying causes. Here are some common causes of distractions:

Technology and digital devices: The proliferation of smart-phones, social media, and constant connectivity has made it easier than ever to be distracted. Notifications, emails, and the lure of scrolling through social media feeds can divert our attention away from important tasks.

Open work environments: Open office layouts and shared workspaces can contribute to distractions. Noise, conversations, and visual distractions can disrupt concentration and make it challenging to focus on work.

Lack of boundaries: Failing to establish clear boundaries between work and personal life can lead to distractions. Mixing work-related tasks with personal activities or allowing personal commitments to interfere with work can result in decreased focus and productivity.

Procrastination: Procrastination is a common cause of distractions. When faced with challenging or unpleasant tasks, we may seek distractions as a way to avoid the work at hand. Procrastination can lead to a cycle of distractions and further delays in completing important tasks.

Internal distractions: Internal distractions, such as negative thoughts, worries, or daydreaming, can also disrupt our focus. Intrusive thoughts or concerns about unrelated matters can divert our attention and make it difficult to concentrate on the task at hand.

STRATEGIES FOR MANAGING DISTRACTIONS

Effectively managing distractions requires a proactive and intentional approach. Here are practical strategies to help you minimize distractions and maintain focus:

Create a Distraction-Free Environment

Designate a dedicated workspace that is free from distractions as much as possible. Minimize noise by using noise-cancelling headphones or playing background music that helps you concentrate. Remove or minimize visual distractions by organizing your workspace and keeping it clutter-free.

Establish Boundaries

Set clear boundaries between work and personal life to prevent distractions from encroaching on your focused time. Communicate your availability to colleagues, family members, and friends, and establish specific periods of uninterrupted work time. Use tools like email auto responders or status updates to communicate your availability and reduce interruptions.

Manage Technology Usage

- Take control of your technology usage to reduce distractions. Here are some strategies:
- Turn off unnecessary notifications on your devices to minimize interruptions.
- Designate specific times to check emails, messages, and social media, rather than constantly reacting to incoming notifications.
- Use website-blocking applications or browser extensions to temporarily block access to distracting websites or social media platforms during focused work periods.
- Practice digital detoxes or designated technology-free periods to allow yourself uninterrupted time for deep work and reflection.

Prioritize and Focus on One Task at a Time

Multitasking can be a significant source of distractions. Instead of attempting to juggle multiple tasks simultaneously, prioritize and focus on one task at a time. Give your full attention to the task at hand, complete it, and then move on to the next one. This focused approach enhances productivity and minimizes distractions caused by switching between tasks.

Practice Time Blocking

Implement time blocking techniques, as discussed in Chapter 12, to allocate specific time blocks for different activities. By designating focused time blocks for specific tasks, you can minimize interruptions and distractions, knowing that you have allocated dedicated time for each activity.

Combat Procrastination

Procrastination is a significant source of distractions. Overcome procrastination by breaking tasks into smaller, manageable steps, setting deadlines for each step, and using techniques like the Pomodoro Technique to work in focused bursts with short breaks in between. By taking proactive steps to combat procrastination, you can minimize distractions and improve productivity.

Practice Mindfulness and Meditation

Cultivating mindfulness and incorporating meditation into your routine can help reduce distractions and improve focus. Mindfulness allows you to become aware of distractions as they arise and gently bring your attention back to the present moment. Regular meditation practice enhances your ability to maintain focus and resist distractions.

Practice the 5-Second Rule

The 5-Second Rule, popularized by Mel Robbins, involves counting backward from five whenever you feel the urge to succumb to distractions. By counting backward and taking action before reaching zero, you interrupt the impulse to be distracted and redirect your focus back to the task at hand.

Utilize Productivity Tools and Techniques

Explore productivity tools and techniques that can help manage distractions and improve focus. Here are some examples:

- To-do list apps or task management tools can help you prioritize and track your tasks, reducing mental clutter and distractions.
- Productivity apps with features like focus timers or white noise generators can help create an optimal work environment and minimize external distractions.
- The Eisenhower Matrix, a time management tool, can assist in prioritizing tasks and identifying those that are important but not urgent, reducing the risk of distractions from less critical activities.

Take Regular Breaks

While it may seem counterintuitive, taking regular breaks can actually help manage distractions. Breaks allow you to recharge, refresh your mind, and maintain focus over an extended period. Incorporate short breaks into your schedule and use them to stretch, walk, or engage in activities that help you relax and rejuvenate.

MAINTAINING FOCUS IN A DIGITAL WORLD

The digital world presents unique challenges when it comes to managing distractions. Here are additional strategies to help you maintain focus amidst digital distractions:

Create a Digital Detox Routine

Implement regular digital detoxes to temporarily disconnect from technology and reduce digital distractions. Designate specific periods or days where you refrain from using digital devices and focus on offline activities, such as reading, exercising, or spending time in nature.

Use Digital Well-being Features

Many devices and applications now offer digital well-being features to help manage distractions. Take advantage of these features, such as screen time limits, app timers, or grayscale mode, to consciously regulate your technology usage and reduce distractions.

Establish Technology-Free Zones

Designate specific areas or periods in your day as technology-free zones. For example, create device-free zones in your bedroom or during meals to promote quality sleep and mindful eating. Establishing boundaries with technology helps create opportunities for focused and distraction-free time.

Practice Single-Tasking

Instead of constantly switching between tasks and devices, practice single-tasking. Focus on one device or one application at a time, minimizing the temptation to multitask or succumb to distractions from multiple sources.

Cultivate Digital Mindfulness

Develop a mindful approach to your digital interactions. Before engaging with technology, ask yourself if it aligns with your goals or if it is a potential source of distraction. Be intentional in your technology usage, focusing on meaningful and purposeful activities rather than mindless scrolling or excessive screen time.

CREATING A DISTRACTION-RESISTANT MINDSET

Managing distractions is not only about implementing external strategies but also about cultivating a mindset that resists distractions. Here are mindset shifts to help you develop a distraction-resistant approach:

Embrace the Power of Deep Work

Recognize the value of deep work, which involves sustained periods of focused, uninterrupted work. Embrace the idea that deep work leads to greater productivity, quality, and satisfaction, and make it a priority in your schedule.

Practice Intentional Focus

Approach your tasks with intention and purpose. Before starting a task, set a clear intention and remind yourself of its importance. This intentional focus helps anchor your attention and strengthens your resolve to resist distractions.

Cultivate Patience and Delay Gratification

Distractions often provide immediate gratification, whereas meaningful work requires patience and delayed gratification. Cultivate patience by reminding yourself of the long-term rewards and benefits of staying focused on important tasks. Embrace the satisfaction that comes from completing meaningful work rather than succumbing to short-term distractions.

Adopt a Growth Mindset

Adopt a growth mindset and view distractions as opportunities for growth and self-improvement. Learn from moments of distraction, reflect on the underlying triggers, and identify strategies to prevent or manage similar situations in the future.

Practice Self-Compassion

Be compassionate with yourself when distractions arise. Rather than dwelling on self-judgment or guilt, acknowledge the distraction, let it go, and refocus on the task at hand. Practice self-compassion by treating yourself with kindness and understanding, allowing you to bounce back from distractions more effectively.

CREATING A DISTRACTION-FREE FUTURE

In a world filled with distractions, creating a distraction-free future requires conscious effort and ongoing commitment. Here are some final thoughts to guide you:

- Embrace the mindset that your time and attention are precious resources, worthy of protection and intentional allocation.
- Regularly assess your environment, routines, and habits to identify potential sources of distractions and make adjustments accordingly.
- Surround yourself with like-minded individuals who value focus and productivity, and encourage each other to minimize distractions.
- Continuously refine your strategies for managing

distractions, experimenting with new techniques and adapting to evolving circumstances.

- Celebrate your successes in managing distractions and acknowledge the positive impact it has on your productivity, well-being, and overall quality of life.

By adopting these strategies and cultivating a distraction-resistant mindset, you can overcome the challenges posed by distractions and make significant strides towards valuing your time and achieving your goals. In the next chapter, we will explore effective strategies for setting and achieving meaningful goals, empowering you to make the most of your limited time and resources.

Chapter 14: Efficient Communication

Effective communication is essential for productivity, collaboration, and building meaningful relationships. In this chapter, we will explore the importance of efficient communication, common communication challenges, and practical strategies for improving communication skills. By becoming a more efficient communicator, you can save time, avoid misunderstandings, and enhance your overall effectiveness in both personal and professional interactions.

THE VALUE OF EFFICIENT COMMUNICATION

Efficient communication is the cornerstone of successful interactions. It ensures that messages are conveyed clearly, accurately, and in a timely manner. Here are some key benefits of efficient communication:

Time savings: Efficient communication saves time by eliminating unnecessary back-and-forth, clarifications, or misunderstandings. Clear and concise messages allow recipients to understand and act upon the information quickly, resulting in increased productivity.

Improved productivity: When communication is efficient, tasks can be completed more effectively and promptly. Clear instructions and expectations enable individuals and teams to work efficiently, minimizing delays and maximizing output.

Enhanced collaboration: Efficient communication fosters collaboration by ensuring that team members are aligned, well-informed, and able to coordinate their efforts seamlessly. It facilitates effective problem-solving, decision-making, and knowledge sharing among team members.

Reduced conflicts and misunderstandings: Efficient communication reduces the likelihood of misunderstandings, conflicts, and errors caused by miscommunication. Clear and concise messages minimize ambiguity and provide clarity, preventing unnecessary complications and disputes.

Strengthened relationships: Effective communication builds trust and strengthens relationships. When individuals communicate efficiently, they convey respect, attentiveness, and a willingness to listen. This fosters positive connections and establishes a supportive and collaborative environment.

Increased influence and persuasion: Efficient communication enables individuals to convey their ideas, opinions, and requests persuasively. It helps to capture the attention of others, articulate compelling arguments, and influence decision-making processes effectively.

COMMON COMMUNICATION CHALLENGES

Communication can be complex, and various challenges can hinder efficiency. It is important to be aware of these challenges and develop strategies to overcome them. Here are some common communication challenges:

Lack of clarity:

Unclear messages, vague instructions, or ambiguous language can lead to misunderstandings and confusion. Lack of clarity can result from poor articulation, assumptions about the recipient's knowledge, or inadequate attention to detail.

Information overload:

In today's digital age, we are bombarded with a constant stream of information. Sorting through the noise and identifying the essential messages can be overwhelming and time-consuming.

Poor listening skills:

Effective communication is a two-way process that requires active listening. Poor listening skills, such as interrupting, not paying attention, or pre-judging, can hinder understanding and lead to miscommunication.

Language barriers:

In multicultural or international settings, language barriers can pose significant challenges to efficient communication. Differences in language proficiency, accents, or cultural nuances may result in misinterpretations and misunderstandings.

Nonverbal communication:

Nonverbal cues, such as body language, facial expressions, and tone of voice, play a crucial role in communication. However, they can be easily misinterpreted or overlooked, leading to misunderstandings or incorrect assumptions.

Digital communication challenges

Communication through digital channels, such as emails or instant messaging, presents its own set of challenges. The absence of nonverbal cues, delayed responses, and the potential for misinterpretation can hinder efficient communication.

STRATEGIES FOR EFFICIENT COMMUNICATION

To enhance your communication skills and promote efficiency, consider the following strategies:

Be Clear and Concise

Ensure that your messages are clear, concise, and easy to understand. Use simple language, avoid jargon or technical terms when communicating with non-experts, and provide specific details or instructions. Eliminate unnecessary information and focus on conveying the essential points.

Adapt to Your Audience

Tailor your communication style and language to suit your audience. Consider their background knowledge, language proficiency, and cultural context. Adapt your message to their needs and preferences, ensuring that it is accessible and understandable to them.

Active Listening

Practice active listening to improve understanding and demonstrate attentiveness. Maintain eye contact, ask clarifying questions, and avoid interrupting. Show genuine interest in what the other person is saying, and paraphrase or summarize their points to confirm your understanding.

Choose the Right Communication Channel

Select the most appropriate communication channel for each situation. While face-to-face conversations are often ideal for complex or sensitive topics, other channels such as email, phone calls, or video conferencing may be more suitable depending on factors such as urgency, convenience, and the need for documentation.

Consider the Timing

Be mindful of the timing when communicating. Avoid sending non-urgent messages outside of regular working hours, unless necessary. Respect others' schedules and priorities, and ensure that your communication does not disrupt their workflow or cause unnecessary distractions.

Practice Empathy and Emotional Intelligence

Embrace empathy and emotional intelligence in your communication. Consider the emotions and perspectives of others, and respond with sensitivity and understanding. Emotional intelligence helps build rapport, enhances listening skills, and fosters meaningful connections with others.

Use Visual Aids

Incorporate visual aids, such as charts, diagrams, or presentations, to support your verbal communication. Visuals can enhance understanding, simplify complex concepts, and provide a visual reference for the information you are conveying.

Seek Clarification

If you receive a message that is unclear or ambiguous, don't hesitate to seek clarification. Ask specific questions to ensure that you fully understand the message and the sender's intentions. By seeking clarification, you can avoid misunderstandings and promote efficient communication.

Practice Mindful Digital Communication

When communicating digitally, be mindful of your tone and language. Avoid the use of excessive capitalization, abbreviations, or emojis that may be misinterpreted. Take time to review and proofread your messages before sending them to ensure accuracy and clarity.

Provide Timely Responses

Respond to messages and requests in a timely manner. Even if you cannot provide a full response immediately, acknowledge the message and provide an estimated timeline for a more comprehensive reply. Prompt responses demonstrate professionalism, respect, and a commitment to efficient communication.

Seek Feedback

Regularly seek feedback on your communication skills to identify areas for improvement. Ask colleagues, mentors, or trusted individuals for their observations and suggestions. Actively seek opportunities to develop your communication skills through workshops, courses, or reading relevant resources.

NURTURING EFFECTIVE COMMUNICATION IN TEAMS

Efficient communication is crucial for successful teamwork and collaboration. Here are strategies to promote effective communication within teams:

Establish Communication Guidelines

Create clear communication guidelines or protocols within your team. Establish expectations regarding response times, preferred channels, and guidelines for meetings or discussions. Ensure that team members are aware of these guidelines and have access to relevant resources or tools.

Foster an Open and Inclusive Environment

Promote open and inclusive communication within the team. Encourage all team members to share their ideas, opinions, and concerns. Create a safe space for respectful discussions and active participation, allowing diverse perspectives to be heard and considered.

Encourage Regular Check-Ins and Feedback

Schedule regular team check-ins to provide updates, address questions, and discuss progress. This check-ins can be in the form of meetings, video conferences, or virtual collaboration platforms. Encourage team members to provide constructive feedback, allowing for continuous improvement in communication and teamwork.

Cultivate Trust and Psychological Safety

Build trust within the team by fostering a culture of psychological safety. Encourage open dialogue, promote constructive feedback, and create an environment where team members feel comfortable expressing their thoughts and concerns. Trust and psychological safety are essential for effective communication and collaboration.

Utilize Collaboration Tools

Leverage technology and collaboration tools to facilitate efficient communication within the team. Project management platforms, messaging apps, and shared document repositories can enhance information sharing, coordination, and remote collaboration.

Clarify Roles and Responsibilities

Clearly define roles and responsibilities within the team to avoid confusion and miscommunication. Ensure that each team member understands their role and knows whom to approach for specific tasks or information. Clarity in roles promotes efficiency and minimizes potential communication gaps.

Practice Active Meeting Management

Make meetings more efficient and productive by practicing active meeting management techniques. Set clear objectives, create agendas, and share relevant materials in advance. Facilitate the discussion, encourage participation, and ensure that decisions and action items are documented and communicated effectively.

OVERCOMING COMMUNICATION BARRIERS

Despite our best efforts, communication barriers can still arise. Here are strategies to help overcome common communication barriers:

Cultivate Patience and Empathy

Be patient when faced with communication challenges. Avoid jumping to conclusions or becoming frustrated. Cultivate empathy and try to understand the perspective of the other person. Patience and empathy contribute to creating a positive and conducive environment for effective communication.

Seek Common Ground

When faced with differences in opinions or perspectives, seek common ground. Look for shared goals or interests that can bridge the gap and facilitate understanding. Find points of agreement and build upon them to foster a constructive and collaborative dialogue.

Ask for Clarification

If you encounter language barriers or misunderstandings, ask for clarification. Request the other person to rephrase or provide additional context to ensure mutual understanding. Active listening and seeking clarification demonstrate your commitment to effective communication.

Embrace Diversity and Inclusion

Appreciate the diversity of communication styles and cultural backgrounds within your interactions. Embrace the richness that different perspectives bring to the table. Be open to learning from others and adapting your communication approach to accommodate different communication preferences.

Provide Constructive Feedback

When faced with ineffective communication, provide constructive feedback to the individuals involved. Offer specific examples and suggestions for improvement, focusing on the behavior or message rather than the person. Constructive feedback helps foster growth and development in communication skills.

CONTINUOUS GROWTH IN COMMUNICATION

Efficient communication is an ongoing journey of growth and improvement. Here are some final thoughts to guide you:

- Cultivate self-awareness by regularly reflecting on your communication style and its impact on others. Be open to feedback and actively seek opportunities for self-improvement.

- Embrace continuous learning by exploring resources, books, or courses on effective communication. Develop a growth mindset that values constant development and improvement in communication skills.
- Practice empathy not only in your communication with others but also in your self-talk. Be compassionate with yourself when faced with communication challenges, and view them as opportunities for growth and learning.
- Seek mentorship or coaching from individuals who excel in communication. Learn from their experiences, observe their techniques, and apply their insights to your own communication practices.
- Remember that effective communication is a two-way process. Be receptive to feedback, actively listen, and adapt your communication style based on the needs and preferences of others.

By implementing these strategies and committing to continuous growth in communication, you can become a more efficient and effective communicator. In the next chapter, we will explore strategies for effective decision-making, empowering you to make informed choices and optimize your use of time and resources.

CHAPTER 15: HEALTHY WORK-LIFE BALANCE

In our modern, fast-paced world, achieving a healthy work-life balance has become increasingly challenging. Many individuals find themselves caught in a perpetual cycle of work-related responsibilities, often neglecting their personal lives and overall well-being. In this chapter, we will delve into the importance of a healthy work-life balance, the detrimental effects of an imbalance, and practical strategies to help you achieve and maintain equilibrium between your professional and personal life.

UNDERSTANDING WORK-LIFE BALANCE

Work-life balance refers to the equilibrium between your professional obligations and personal well-being. It involves allocating time and energy to various aspects of your life, including work, family, relationships, personal growth, and leisure activities. Achieving a healthy work-life balance allows you to pursue both professional success and personal fulfillment, leading to overall satisfaction and well-being.

THE IMPORTANCE OF A HEALTHY WORK-LIFE BALANCE

Maintaining a healthy work-life balance is essential for several *reasons:*

Physical and mental well-being: A healthy work-life balance contributes to your overall physical and mental health. It allows you to prioritize self-care activities, such as exercise, proper nutrition, and sufficient rest, which are crucial for maintaining energy, reducing stress, and preventing burnout.

Enhanced productivity and performance: When you strike a balance between work and personal life, you are better equipped to focus and perform at your best. Taking breaks, engaging in leisure activities, and spending quality time with loved ones rejuvenate your mind and improve your cognitive abilities, leading to increased productivity and higher quality work.

Improved relationships: A healthy work-life balance nurtures meaningful relationships. It allows you to dedicate time and attention to your family, friends, and loved ones, fostering stronger connections and a support system. Healthy relationships provide emotional well-being and contribute to a sense of fulfillment and happiness.

Personal growth and fulfillment: Balancing work and personal life provides opportunities for personal growth and fulfillment. Pursuing hobbies, interests, and personal goals outside of work expands your horizons, enhances your skills, and brings a sense of accomplishment. It adds depth and richness to your life beyond professional achievements.

Prevention of burnout: An imbalance between work and personal life can lead to burnout, a state of chronic physical and emotional exhaustion. Burnout can result in decreased motivation, increased cynicism, and diminished performance. Maintaining a healthy work-life balance helps prevent burnout and promotes sustainable long-term success.

SIGNS OF AN IMBALANCE

It is important to recognize the signs of an imbalance between work and personal life. Here are some common indicators that you may need to reassess your work-life balance:

Feeling constantly overwhelmed or stressed: If you find yourself consistently overwhelmed by work-related demands and unable to relax or enjoy personal activities, it may be a sign of an imbalance.

Neglected personal relationships: When work takes precedence over your personal relationships, causing strain or neglect, it indicates an imbalance. Lack of quality time with loved ones can lead to feelings of isolation and dissatisfaction.

Health issues and fatigue: Frequent illnesses, chronic fatigue, or persistent physical symptoms may be a result of excessive work demands and neglecting self-care.

Loss of interest in hobbies and activities: If you no longer have time or energy for activities you once enjoyed outside of work, it may indicate an imbalance. Losing touch with hobbies and interests can negatively impact your sense of fulfillment and happiness.

Difficulty disconnecting from work: Inability to switch off from work and constant preoccupation with work-related matters, even during personal time, may suggest an imbalance. It becomes challenging to relax and recharge when work dominates your thoughts and actions.

STRATEGIES FOR ACHIEVING A HEALTHY WORK-LIFE BALANCE

To achieve and maintain a healthy work-life balance, consider the following strategies:

Define Your Priorities

Identify your core values, goals, and priorities in both your professional and personal life. Understanding what truly matters to you allows you to allocate your time and energy accordingly. Determine the aspects of your life that are non-negotiable and ensure they receive the attention they deserve.

Set Boundaries

Establish clear boundaries between work and personal life. Communicate your availability to colleagues and clients, and be assertive in protecting your personal time. Avoid excessive overtime or constant accessibility, as it can blur the lines between work and personal life.

Practice Effective Time Management

Develop strong time management skills to optimize your use of time and achieve a balance between work and personal activities. Prioritize tasks, set realistic deadlines, and allocate dedicated time blocks for different activities. Eliminate time-wasting activities and delegate tasks when appropriate.

Learn to Say No

Don't be afraid to say no to requests or commitments that do not align with your priorities or exceed your capacity. Prioritize your well-being and avoid over-committing yourself. Saying no allows you to create space for activities that bring you joy and contribute to your work-life balance.

Delegate and Outsource

Delegate tasks at work and outsource personal responsibilities when possible. Recognize that you cannot do everything alone and seek support from colleagues, family members, or professionals. Delegating and outsourcing allow you to focus on high-value activities and alleviate the pressure of overwhelming workloads.

Establish Rituals and Routines

Create rituals and routines that help you transition between work and personal life. For example, develop a winding-down routine at the end of the workday to signify the transition into personal time. Establishing clear rituals and routines helps your mind and body recognize the boundaries between work and personal life.

Prioritize Self-Care

Make self-care a priority in your life. Engage in activities that promote your physical, mental, and emotional well-being. Exercise regularly, practice mindfulness or meditation, prioritize quality sleep, and engage in activities that bring you joy and relaxation. Nurturing yourself allows you to show up as your best self in both work and personal domains.

Establish Tech-Free Time

Designate specific periods in your day or week as tech-free time. Disconnect from digital devices and immerse yourself in activities that do not involve screens. Embrace the quietude and allow yourself to be present in the moment, free from the constant distractions of technology.

Communicate and Seek Support

Communicate your work-life balance goals and needs with your supervisor, colleagues, and loved ones. Openly discuss expectations and negotiate flexible arrangements when possible. Seek support from your social network, whether it be family, friends, or mentors, to help you maintain a healthy work-life balance.

Regularly Evaluate and Adjust

Regularly assess your work-life balance and make adjustments as needed. Evaluate the effectiveness of your strategies, reflect on your satisfaction and well-being, and make necessary changes to align with your evolving needs and priorities.

OVERCOMING WORK-LIFE BALANCE CHALLENGES

Challenges may arise while striving for a healthy work-life balance. Here are strategies to help you overcome common challenges:

Combating Guilt

Let go of guilt associated with prioritizing personal time or setting boundaries. Remember that taking care of yourself and nurturing personal relationships is vital for overall well-being and sustainable success. Acknowledge that you deserve to have a fulfilling life outside of work.

Avoiding the "Always On" Mentality

Resist the temptation to be constantly accessible and responsive to work-related matters. Embrace the concept of "off" time and establish periods of rest and rejuvenation. Switch off email notifications and set clear expectations with colleagues regarding your availability outside of working hours.

Seeking Support from Others

If you are struggling to achieve work-life balance, seek support from trusted individuals. Talk to mentors, colleagues, or loved ones who can offer guidance, perspective, or practical advice. Sharing your challenges and experiences with others can provide valuable insights and support.

Embracing Flexibility

Recognize that achieving a perfect balance between work and personal life may be unrealistic at times. Embrace the concept of flexibility and adjust your expectations accordingly. Some periods may require more focused attention on work, while others may allow for greater personal time. Flexibility allows you to navigate the ebb and flow of life more gracefully.

SUSTAINING A HEALTHY WORK-LIFE BALANCE

Maintaining a healthy work-life balance is an ongoing process that requires commitment and self-awareness. Here are some final thoughts to guide you:

- Regularly assess and reassess your work-life balance to

ensure that it aligns with your evolving needs, goals, and priorities.

- Cultivate self-awareness by regularly reflecting on your satisfaction, energy levels, and overall well-being. Pay attention to any warning signs of an imbalance and take proactive steps to address them.
- Communicate openly and honestly with your employer, colleagues, and loved ones about your work-life balance goals and needs. Collaboration and support from others are crucial for sustaining a healthy balance.
- Be adaptable and willing to adjust your strategies as circumstances change. Flexibility allows you to navigate the complexities of work and personal life more effectively.
- Remember that work-life balance is a deeply personal journey. It may look different for each individual. Focus on what brings you fulfillment, joy, and a sense of well-being.

By implementing these strategies and cultivating a healthy work-life balance, you can experience greater satisfaction, well-being, and success in both your professional and personal life. In the next chapter, we will explore the art of effective decision-making, empowering you to make informed choices and optimize your use of time and resources.

CHAPTER 16: MINDFULNESS AND TIME AWARENESS

I n our fast-paced and hectic lives, it's easy to get caught up in the never-ending demands and distractions that surround us. We often find ourselves rushing from one task to another, feeling overwhelmed and disconnected from the present moment. In this chapter, we will explore the concepts of mindfulness and time awareness and their profound impact on our ability to value and make the most of our limited time.

UNDERSTANDING MINDFULNESS

Mindfulness is the practice of being fully present and engaged in the current moment, with an open and non-judgmental attitude. It involves paying deliberate attention to our thoughts, feelings, bodily sensations, and the surrounding environment. By cultivating mindfulness, we can develop a heightened sense of awareness and bring a sense of clarity and focus to our experiences.

THE POWER OF MINDFULNESS IN TIME MANAGEMENT

Mindfulness plays a crucial role in time management and our relationship with time. By incorporating mindfulness into our daily lives, we can:

Cultivate Present-Moment Awareness: Mindfulness brings our attention to the present moment, allowing us to fully engage with the task at hand. By focusing on the present, we can minimize distractions, improve concentration, and enhance our efficiency and productivity.

Reduce Mental Clutter: Mindfulness helps us become aware of and detach from unhelpful thoughts, worries, and mental clutter that often consume our time and energy. By letting go of unnecessary mental baggage, we create space for clear thinking and effective decision-making.

Enhance Time Perception: When we practice mindfulness, our perception of time expands. We become more attuned to the passing of time, allowing us to make conscious choices about how we allocate our time and prioritize our activities.

Reduce Procrastination: Mindfulness helps us recognize and overcome the habit of procrastination. By being present and aware of our intentions and motivations, we can more easily identify and address the underlying causes of procrastination, such as fear, perfectionism, or lack of clarity.

Improve Time Quality: Mindfulness allows us to savor and appreciate the present moment, enhancing the quality of our experiences. By being fully engaged and attentive, we can derive greater satisfaction, fulfillment, and meaning from the activities we undertake.

TECHNIQUES FOR CULTIVATING MINDFULNESS

To incorporate mindfulness into your daily life and enhance your time awareness, consider the following techniques:

Mindful Breathing

Breathing is an anchor to the present moment. Take regular pauses throughout the day to focus on your breath. Notice the sensation of the breath entering and leaving your body.

Whenever your mind wanders, gently bring your attention back to the breath, cultivating a sense of calm and presence.

Body Scan Meditation

Engage in a body scan meditation to develop a deeper connection with your body and physical sensations. Start at the top of your head and gradually move your attention down, observing any sensations or tensions in each part of your body. This practice promotes relaxation, body awareness, and grounding in the present moment.

Mindful Observation

Take a few minutes to observe your surroundings with curiosity and openness. Notice the colors, shapes, textures, and sounds around you. Engage your senses fully, without judgment or analysis. This practice enhances your ability to be fully present in the current moment and cultivates a sense of appreciation for the world around you.

Mindful Eating

Slow down and bring mindfulness to your meals. Pay attention to the taste, texture, and aroma of the food. Chew slowly and savor each bite. Notice the sensations of hunger and fullness. By practicing mindful eating, you can cultivate a healthier relationship with food and enjoy the nourishment it provides.

Mindful Technology Use

Bring mindfulness to your interactions with technology. Before reaching for your phone or engaging in digital activities, pause and ask yourself if it aligns with your intentions and priorities. Set boundaries around technology usage and be fully present in your interactions, avoiding mindless scrolling or excessive screen time.

Mindful Movement

Engage in mindful movement practices such as yoga, tai chi, or walking meditation. Pay attention to the sensations, movements, and breathe as you engage in these activities. By combining movement with mindfulness, you can cultivate a greater sense of body awareness, relaxation, and mental clarity.

Mindful Transitions

Bring mindfulness to the transitions between different activities or roles in your day. Take a moment to pause, breathe, and intentionally shift your focus and energy. By consciously acknowledging and transitioning between tasks, you can bring a sense of presence and intentionality to each activity.

CULTIVATING TIME AWARENESS

In addition to mindfulness, developing time awareness is essential for valuing and making the most of our limited time. Time awareness involves:

Conscious Time Perception: Pay attention to how you perceive time in different contexts. Notice when time seems to fly by, and when it feels slow and stretched. By developing a deeper awareness of time, you can align your activities with your natural rhythms and make conscious choices about how you allocate your time.

Time Tracking: Track your time for a period to gain insight into how you spend your days. Use a journal, digital tool, or time-tracking app to record your activities and the amount of time you allocate to each. This practice helps identify patterns, time sinks, and areas where adjustments can be made.

Prioritization and Time Allocation: Develop the habit of regularly assessing your priorities and consciously allocating time to them. Identify your most important tasks and ensure they receive dedicated time blocks in your schedule. By aligning your time with your values and goals, you can make deliberate choices and avoid getting caught up in unimportant or time-consuming activities.

Time-Boxing: Use the technique of time-boxing to create

focused periods of work. Set specific time intervals for tasks or activities, and commit to working on them exclusively during that time. By working within defined time frames, you can improve your focus, productivity, and accountability.

Time Boundaries: Establish clear boundaries around your time to protect your work-life balance. Communicate your availability and establish specific periods for work, personal activities, and rest. Respect these boundaries and assertively communicate them to others, enabling you to maintain control over how you spend your time.

APPLYING MINDFULNESS AND TIME AWARENESS IN DAILY LIFE

To apply mindfulness and time awareness effectively in your daily life, consider the following strategies:

Morning Rituals

Start your day with mindfulness practices that ground you in the present moment. Engage in activities such as meditation, journaling, or setting intentions for the day. By beginning your day mindfully, you can set a positive tone and cultivate an awareness that carries through the rest of your activities.

Single-Tasking

Practice single-tasking by focusing on one activity at a time. Avoid multitasking, as it divides your attention and diminishes the quality of your work. By immersing yourself fully in one task, you can achieve a state of flow and enhance your efficiency and effectiveness.

Regular Check-Ins

Take regular check-in breaks throughout the day to assess your mental and emotional state. Pause, breathe, and inquire into how you are feeling and what you need in that moment. This practice helps you realign your focus, address any distractions or stressors, and make conscious decisions about how to proceed.

End-of-Day Reflection

Engage in an end-of-day reflection to review your activities, accomplishments, and areas for improvement. Celebrate your successes and acknowledge the efforts you put forth. Reflect on how effectively you managed your time and identify any adjustments or learnings for the future.

Mindful Transitions

Bring mindfulness to the transitions between work and personal life, allowing yourself a moment to mentally shift gears. Use rituals or activities such as deep breathing, stretching, or a short walk to create a clear boundary between different domains of your life. By bringing conscious awareness to these transitions, you can maintain balance and prevent the blending of work and personal time.

Digital Detox

Periodically disconnect from digital devices and create tech-free periods in your day or week. Use this time to engage in activities that promote mindfulness, such as reading, spending time in nature, or engaging in creative pursuits. By unplugging from technology, you can reduce distractions and create space for present-moment awareness.

EMBRACING THE PRESENT MOMENT

In a world that often glorifies busyness and constant productivity, it is essential to remember the value of embracing the present moment. By cultivating mindfulness and time awareness, you can develop a deep appreciation for the limited nature of time and the importance of making conscious choices about how you spend it.

Remember, time is a precious resource that cannot be replenished. By valuing and making the most of your time through mindfulness and time awareness, you can experience greater fulfillment, productivity, and well-being in both your personal and professional life. In the next chapter, we will explore strategies for maintaining focus and concentration, empowering you to maximize your productivity and accomplish your goals effectively.

CHAPTER 17: MAXIMIZING PRODUCTIVITY

I n today's fast-paced world, the ability to maximize productivity is crucial for achieving success and making the most of our limited time. Productivity goes beyond simply being busy; it involves effectively managing our tasks, utilizing our resources, and accomplishing our goals in a focused and efficient manner. In this chapter, we will explore strategies and techniques for maximizing productivity and optimizing our use of time.

UNDERSTANDING PRODUCTIVITY

Productivity refers to the ability to accomplish tasks, achieve goals, and produce desired outcomes efficiently. It involves effectively managing our time, energy, and resources to accomplish meaningful work. By maximizing productivity, we can increase our efficiency, achieve more in less time, and create a sense of accomplishment and satisfaction.

THE IMPORTANCE OF MAXIMIZING PRODUCTIVITY

Maximizing productivity is essential for several reasons:

Optimal Resource Utilization: By maximizing productivity, we make the most efficient use of our resources, including time, energy, and skills. This allows us to accomplish more with the same amount of resources, leading to increased effectiveness and output.

Goal Achievement: Productivity is directly linked to goal achievement. When we maximize our productivity, we move closer to our goals, accomplish tasks in a timely manner, and experience a sense of progress and fulfillment.

Time Management: Maximizing productivity involves effective time management. By prioritizing tasks, eliminating distractions, and focusing on high-value activities, we can make the most of our time and avoid wasting it on unproductive tasks or activities.

Reduced Stress and Overwhelm: Productivity helps reduce stress and overwhelm by providing a sense of control and accomplishment. When we manage our tasks effectively and make progress towards our goals, we experience less stress and feel more in control of our responsibilities.

Increased Quality: Maximizing productivity allows us to allocate more time and attention to each task, resulting in increased quality and attention to detail. By avoiding rushed or haphazard work, we can produce higher-quality outcomes.

STRATEGIES FOR MAXIMIZING PRODUCTIVITY

To maximize productivity and make the most of your time, consider implementing the following strategies:

Set Clear Goals

Start by setting clear, specific, and measurable goals. Define what you want to accomplish and break down your goals into smaller, manageable tasks. Clear goals provide direction and focus, allowing you to prioritize your efforts effectively.

Prioritize Tasks

Prioritize your tasks based on their importance and urgency. Use techniques such as the Eisenhower Matrix, which categorizes tasks into four quadrants: urgent and important, important but not urgent, urgent but not important, and neither urgent nor important. Focus your energy on high-priority tasks that align with your goals.

Plan and Organize

Develop a daily or weekly plan that outlines your tasks, deadlines, and commitments. Use productivity tools, such as calendars, to schedule your activities and allocate specific time blocks for different tasks. Organize your workspace, digital files, and resources to minimize distractions and optimize efficiency.

Manage Time Effectively

Practice effective time management techniques, such as time blocking or the Pomodoro Technique. Time blocking involves dedicating specific time periods to specific tasks, while the Pomodoro Technique involves working in focused bursts of time followed by short breaks. Experiment with different time management approaches to find what works best for you.

Minimize Distractions

Identify and minimize distractions that hinder your productivity. This may involve turning off notifications on your phone, using website blockers to prevent access to distracting websites, or creating a dedicated workspace free from interruptions. Take control of your environment to create a focused and distraction-free zone.

Practice Effective Decision-Making

Indecision and decision fatigue can drain your productivity. Practice effective decision-making by gathering necessary information, setting clear criteria, and making timely choices. Avoid overthinking or getting stuck in analysis paralysis, as this can impede progress and waste valuable time.

Harness the Power of Habits

Develop productive habits that support your goals and

streamline your workflow. Create a routine that incorporates regular, productive habits, such as reviewing your tasks and priorities, practicing mindfulness, or engaging in physical activity. By automating certain aspects of your day, you reduce the need for decision-making and conserve mental energy.

Delegate and Outsource

Recognize that you cannot do everything alone. Delegate tasks that can be handled by others and outsource non-core activities or tasks that are not your strengths. Effective delegation and outsourcing free up your time and energy to focus on high-value activities that require your expertise.

Focus on Deep Work

Deep work refers to focused, uninterrupted, and high-concentration work on cognitively demanding tasks. Create dedicated blocks of time for deep work, free from distractions. Turn off notifications, close unnecessary tabs or applications, and immerse yourself in the task at hand. Deep work allows you to achieve a state of flow and maximize your productivity.

Practice Energy Management

Manage your energy levels by prioritizing activities that align with your natural energy patterns. Identify your peak energy times and schedule your most important or challenging tasks during those periods. Take regular breaks, engage in physical activity, and nourish your body with nutritious food and sufficient rest to sustain your energy levels throughout the day.

Embrace Continuous Learning

Commit to continuous learning and personal development. Invest time in expanding your knowledge and acquiring new skills that can enhance your productivity. Stay updated on industry trends, technologies, and best practices to optimize your workflow and stay ahead.

Regularly Evaluate and Reflect

Regularly evaluate your productivity strategies and reflect on your progress. Assess what works well for you and what needs adjustment. Identify any bottlenecks or areas for improvement in your workflow and make necessary changes to enhance your productivity.

OVERCOMING PRODUCTIVITY CHALLENGES

Maximizing productivity can come with its own set of challenges. Here are strategies to help you overcome common productivity challenges:

Overcoming Procrastination

Procrastination can hinder productivity. Combat it by breaking tasks into smaller, manageable steps, setting deadlines, and creating accountability mechanisms. Use techniques such as the "two-minute rule" or "eat the frog" method to tackle tasks promptly and build momentum.

Managing Overwhelm

Feeling overwhelmed can lead to a decline in productivity. Break down complex tasks into smaller, more manageable parts. Prioritize tasks and focus on one task at a time to avoid becoming overwhelmed by the sheer volume of work. Seek support or delegate tasks when necessary.

Handling Perfectionism

Perfectionism can be a productivity roadblock. Set realistic expectations and recognize that perfection is often unattainable. Embrace the concept of "good enough" and focus on progress rather than perfection. Celebrate your achievements along the way.

Dealing with Multitasking

Multitasking can decrease productivity and quality of work.

Practice single-tasking by focusing on one task at a time. Minimize distractions and give each task your full attention and effort. By focusing on one task at a time, you can complete it more efficiently and effectively.

SUSTAINABLE PRODUCTIVITY

To ensure sustainable productivity, it is important to consider the following factors:

Work-Life Balance

Maintain a healthy work-life balance to avoid burnout and sustain long-term productivity. Prioritize self-care, engage in activities that rejuvenate you, and allocate time for rest and relaxation. Remember that productivity is not solely about work but also about maintaining overall well-being.

Self-Reflection and Adjustment

Regularly reflect on your productivity strategies and assess their effectiveness. Be willing to make adjustments and try new approaches as needed. Embrace a growth mindset that values continuous improvement and adaptability.

Celebrate Progress and Success

Acknowledge and celebrate your progress and achievements. Recognize the effort you put into your work and the milestones you reach. Celebrating success boosts motivation, morale, and overall productivity.

Work Environment Optimization

Create an environment that supports your productivity. Ensure your workspace is organized, comfortable, and free from distractions. Surround yourself with tools, resources, and visuals that inspire and motivate you. Personalize your workspace to reflect your preferences and create a positive work atmosphere.

Self-Management

Take ownership of your time and tasks. Set boundaries, manage your workload effectively, and communicate your needs and limitations assertively. Be proactive in managing your time, energy, and resources to maintain optimal productivity.

EMBRACING PRODUCTIVITY AS A MINDSET

Maximizing productivity is not just about implementing strategies; it is a mindset and a conscious choice to be intentional with your time and efforts. By adopting a productivity mindset, you can cultivate discipline, focus, and resilience to consistently accomplish your goals and make the most of your limited time.

Remember, productivity is not about being busy; it is about being purposeful and effective. By implementing the strategies outlined in this chapter and adopting a productivity mindset, you can maximize your productivity, achieve your goals, and create a fulfilling and successful life. In the next chapter, we will explore the concept of work-life integration, empowering you to find harmony and synergy between your professional and personal life.

CHAPTER 18: THE POWER OF HABITS

Habits are powerful forces that shape our lives and determine our level of success and satisfaction. From our daily routines to our long-term goals, habits play a significant role in how we spend our time and make the most of our limited resources. In this chapter, we will explore the nature of habits, their impact on our productivity and well-being, and strategies for developing and maintaining positive habits that support our goals and values.

UNDERSTANDING HABITS

Habits are automatic routines or behaviors that we engage in without conscious thought or decision-making. They are deeply ingrained patterns that our brains develop over time as a way to conserve mental energy and streamline our actions. Habits can be both beneficial and detrimental, depending on their nature and impact on our lives.

THE HABIT LOOP

*Habits follow a predictable pattern known as the habit loop, which consists of three stages: **cue, routine, and reward.***

Cue: The cue is a trigger that prompts the brain to initiate a particular behavior. It can be a specific time of day, a visual or auditory stimulus, an emotional state, or a particular location.

The cue signals the brain to start the habit.

Routine: The routine is the behavior itself—the habit that we engage in. It can be a physical action, a mental process, or an emotional response. The routine is the habitual behavior that occurs in response to the cue.

Reward: The reward is the positive reinforcement that follows the completion of the routine. It can be a sense of accomplishment, a feeling of pleasure or relief, or a tangible reward. The reward strengthens the habit loop by providing a satisfying outcome.

Understanding the habit loop is essential for modifying or creating new habits. By identifying the cue, modifying the routine, and providing a satisfying reward, we can shape our habits to align with our goals and values.

THE IMPACT OF HABITS ON PRODUCTIVITY

Habits have a significant impact on our productivity. They shape our daily routines, influence our decision-making, and determine how effectively we manage our time and resources. Here are some ways habits influence productivity:

Automation: Habits allow us to automate certain behaviors, reducing the need for conscious decision-making and conserving mental energy. By automating repetitive tasks or routines, we free up cognitive resources for more complex and creative endeavors.

Consistency: Habits provide consistency and stability in our daily lives. When we establish productive habits, such as a morning routine or a dedicated workspace, we create a structured environment that supports productivity and focus.

Time Management: Habits help us manage our time effectively. By establishing time-management habits, such as planning and prioritizing tasks, we can optimize our use of time and allocate it to high-value activities.

Proactive Behavior: Productive habits promote proactive behavior. When we develop habits that align with our goals, such as regular exercise or setting aside time for learning, we become more proactive in pursuing our aspirations and maximizing our potential.

Focus and Flow: Habits contribute to our ability to achieve a state of focus and flow. By establishing habits that minimize distractions, create a conductive work environment, or promote deep work, we can enter a state of heightened concentration and productivity.

STRATEGIES FOR DEVELOPING POSITIVE HABITS

Developing positive habits is a powerful way to enhance productivity and achieve our goals. Here are strategies for developing and maintaining positive habits:

Identify Keystone Habits

Keystone habits are foundational habits that have a ripple effect on other areas of our lives. Identify keystone habits that can serve as a catalyst for positive change. For example, regular exercise or mindfulness practice can have a positive impact on various aspects of our lives, including our productivity, well-being, and decision-making.

Start Small

Begin by focusing on small, achievable habits. Break down larger goals into smaller, manageable steps. By starting small, we build momentum, increase our chances of success, and create a solid foundation for larger habit changes.

Harness the Power of Triggers

Use triggers or cues to initiate desired habits. Pair the habit you want to develop with an existing cue or establish a new trigger that prompts you to engage in the desired behavior. For example, if you want to develop a reading habit, you can link it to a specific time of day or place.

Create a Supportive Environment

Shape your environment to support your desired habits. Remove or minimize obstacles that hinder habit formation and create visual cues or reminders that prompt the desired behavior. For example, if you want to develop a habit of drinking more water, keep a water bottle visible and easily accessible.

Practice Consistency

Consistency is key to habit formation. Commit to practicing the habit consistently, ideally on a daily basis. Consistency helps reinforce the habit loop and strengthens the neural pathways associated with the desired behavior.

Track Progress

Track your progress to maintain motivation and accountability. Use habit-tracking tools or apps to monitor your adherence to the habit. Celebrate your successes and reflect on any challenges or setbacks to adjust your approach if needed.

Use Habit Stacking

Habit stacking involves linking a new habit to an existing one. Identify a current habit that you already perform consistently and use it as a trigger for the new habit. By stacking habits, you leverage the existing neural pathways associated with the established habit.

Practice Mindfulness

Bring mindfulness to your habits by being fully present and intentional. Notice the cues, routines, and rewards associated with your habits. By cultivating mindfulness, you can make conscious choices about your habits and be more attuned to their impact on your productivity and well-being.

Utilize Implementation Intentions

Use implementation intentions to reinforce habit formation. Create a specific plan that outlines when and where you will engage in the desired behavior. For example, instead of saying, "I will exercise more," state, "I will go for a 30-minute walk in the park every morning at 7 a.m."

Seek Accountability and Support

Engage in accountability and support systems to help maintain positive habits. Share your habit goals with a trusted friend, join a group or community with similar interests, or consider hiring a coach or mentor who can provide guidance and encouragement.

OVERCOMING HABIT CHALLENGES

Developing positive habits can present challenges along the way. Here are strategies for overcoming common habit challenges:

Address Resistance and Obstacles

Identify any resistance or obstacles that hinder habit formation. Explore the underlying reasons for resistance and find ways to address them. This may involve reframing beliefs, seeking support, or adjusting the habit implementation.

Practice Self-Compassion

Be kind to yourself throughout the habit formation process. Recognize that setbacks and slip-ups are natural and part of the learning process. Practice self-compassion by acknowledging your efforts and recommitting to your habit goals.

Focus on Progress, Not Perfection

Shift your focus from perfection to progress. Embrace the idea that habits are developed over time, and it's the cumulative effect of consistent practice that matters. Celebrate small victories and recognize the progress you've made.

Adjust and Refine

Be open to adjusting and refining your habits as needed. Habits are not set in stone and can evolve as your needs and circumstances change. Regularly assess your habits and make adjustments to ensure they continue to support your goals and well-being.

SUSTAINING POSITIVE HABITS

Sustaining positive habits requires ongoing effort and commitment. Here are strategies for maintaining and reinforcing positive habits:

Regular Review and Reflection

Regularly review your habits and reflect on their impact on your productivity and well-being. Assess whether they align with your goals and values. Make any necessary adjustments or additions to your habit repertoire.

Celebrate Milestones

Celebrate milestones and achievements along your habit journey. Acknowledge the progress you've made and reward yourself for your efforts. Celebrating milestones reinforces the positive associations with your habits and motivates you to continue.

Seek Support and Accountability

Engage in ongoing support and accountability to sustain your positive habits. Join a mastermind group, enlist an accountability partner, or participate in habit-tracking communities. Surround yourself with like-minded individuals who can provide encouragement and motivation.

Maintain Self-Care Practices

Prioritize self-care to sustain your habits. Ensure you're getting enough rest, nourishing your body with healthy food, and engaging in activities that promote your overall well-being.

When you take care of yourself, you have the energy and resilience to maintain your positive habits.

Embrace Flexibility

Recognize that life is dynamic, and circumstances may change. Embrace flexibility in your habits and be willing to adapt as needed. Allow for modifications while staying true to the core values and principles that underpin your habits.

EMBRACING THE POWER OF HABITS

Habits are the building blocks of our lives. By understanding the nature of habits, intentionally developing positive habits, and sustaining them over time, we can harness their power to enhance our productivity, well-being, and overall satisfaction.

Remember, habits are not formed overnight, but with consistency and conscious effort, they can transform our lives. By cultivating positive habits that align with our goals and values, we can make the most of our limited time and create a life of purpose, success, and fulfillment. In the next chapter, we will explore the concept of lifelong learning and its role in personal and professional growth.

CHAPTER 19: MANAGING STRESS AND BURNOUT

In our fast-paced and demanding world, stress and burnout have become all too common. The pressure to perform, meet deadlines, and balance multiple responsibilities can take a toll on our well-being and productivity. In this chapter, we will explore the causes and consequences of stress and burnout, as well as strategies for effectively managing them to protect our physical and mental health and optimize our use of time.

UNDERSTANDING STRESS AND BURNOUT

Stress is a natural response to the demands and pressures we face in our daily lives. It can be triggered by various factors, including work-related responsibilities, personal challenges, financial pressures, or relationship difficulties. While some stress can be motivating and help us perform at our best, chronic and excessive stress can have detrimental effects on our well-being.

Burnout, on the other hand, is a state of physical, mental, and emotional exhaustion that results from prolonged exposure to chronic stress. It is characterized by feelings of cynicism, detachment, and a sense of reduced personal accomplishment. Burnout can affect all aspects of our lives, including our work performance, relationships, and overall quality of life.

THE IMPACT OF STRESS AND BURNOUT

Stress and burnout have far-reaching consequences that can negatively impact various areas of our lives. Some of the key impacts include:

Physical Health: Chronic stress and burnout can lead to a range of physical health issues, including increased risk of cardiovascular diseases, weakened immune system, gastrointestinal problems, and sleep disturbances. Prolonged exposure to stress hormones can have long-term effects on our overall health and well-being.

Mental Health: Stress and burnout are closely linked to mental health problems, such as anxiety and depression. The constant pressure and demands can overwhelm our coping mechanisms, leading to feelings of helplessness, irritability, and emotional instability.

Work Performance: Stress and burnout can significantly impact our productivity and performance at work. As burnout progresses, we may experience decreased motivation, difficulty concentrating, and reduced creativity and problem-solving abilities. This can lead to a decline in the quality of our work and hinder our career advancement.

Relationships: Chronic stress and burnout can strain our relationships, both personal and professional. Irritability, emotional exhaustion, and a lack of energy or enthusiasm can affect our ability to connect with others and maintain healthy interactions.

Work-Life Balance: Excessive stress and burnout can disrupt our work-life balance, making it difficult to find time for leisure, relaxation, and self-care. This imbalance can further perpetuate the cycle of stress and burnout, as we neglect the activities and relationships that bring joy and fulfillment to our lives.

STRATEGIES FOR MANAGING STRESS

Effectively managing stress is essential for maintaining our well-being and optimizing our use of time. Here are strategies for managing stress effectively:

Identify Stressors

Start by identifying the specific stressors in your life. Recognize the situations, tasks, or people that contribute to your stress levels. By pinpointing the sources of stress, you can develop targeted strategies to address and manage them.

Prioritize Self-Care

Make self-care a priority in your life. Engage in activities that promote relaxation, rejuvenation, and overall well-being. This can include regular exercise, adequate sleep, healthy eating, and practicing mindfulness or meditation. Taking care of yourself strengthens your resilience and equips you to handle stress more effectively.

Establish Boundaries

Set clear boundaries to protect your time, energy, and well-being. Learn to say no to excessive commitments or tasks that overwhelm you. Establish boundaries around work hours, personal time, and obligations to create a healthy work-life balance.

Time Management

Effective time management can help alleviate stress. Prioritize tasks, set realistic deadlines, and break larger projects into smaller, manageable steps. Use time-blocking techniques to allocate dedicated time for specific activities and create a sense of structure and control in your schedule.

Seek Support

Reach out for support when you're feeling overwhelmed. Talk to trusted friends, family members, or colleagues who can provide a listening ear or offer guidance. Consider seeking professional help, such as therapy or counseling, to develop coping strategies and gain valuable insights into managing stress.

Practice Stress-Relief Techniques

Engage in stress-relief techniques to help manage and reduce stress levels. These can include deep breathing exercises, progressive muscle relaxation, guided imagery, or engaging in hobbies and activities that bring you joy and relaxation. Find techniques that resonate with you and incorporate them into your daily routine.

Foster Healthy Coping Mechanisms

Develop healthy coping mechanisms for dealing with stress. This can include journaling, engaging in creative outlets, practicing gratitude, or seeking social support. Find healthy ways to express and process your emotions rather than resorting to negative coping strategies like substance abuse or excessive screen time.

Manage Workload and Expectations

Assess your workload and manage your commitments and expectations realistically. Learn to delegate tasks when possible and communicate your limitations effectively. Avoid taking on more than you can handle and be willing to renegotiate deadlines or seek additional resources if needed.

Take Regular Breaks

Incorporate regular breaks into your workday to recharge and rejuvenate. Stepping away from work, even for a few minutes, can help reduce stress and improve focus and productivity. Use breaks to engage in activities that relax and energize you, such as stretching, taking a short walk, or practicing mindfulness.

Foster Supportive Relationships

Nurture supportive relationships that provide emotional support and understanding. Surround yourself with positive influences and seek out social connections that uplift and inspire you. Engage in meaningful conversations and share your experiences, as connecting with others can help alleviate stress and foster a sense of belonging.

STRATEGIES FOR PREVENTING BURNOUT

Preventing burnout requires a proactive approach to managing stress and prioritizing self-care. Here are strategies for preventing burnout:

Recognize Warning Signs

Be aware of the early warning signs of burnout, such as chronic fatigue, decreased motivation, irritability, and feelings of cynicism or detachment. By recognizing these signs, you can take steps to address them before burnout escalates.

Create a Supportive Work Environment

Advocate for a supportive work environment that values work-life balance and employee well-being. Encourage open communication, flexible work arrangements, and initiatives that promote employee wellness. Seek out resources and support within your organization to help manage stress and prevent burnout.

Practice Self-Reflection

Regularly reflect on your values, goals, and priorities. Assess whether your current lifestyle aligns with your aspirations and make adjustments as needed. This self-reflection can help you identify potential areas of imbalance or over-commitment that may contribute to burnout.

Develop a Support System

Cultivate a strong support system both inside and outside of work. Surround yourself with colleagues, mentors, or friends who understand the challenges you face and can provide support and encouragement. Participate in professional networks or communities where you can connect with others who share similar experiences.

Engage in Meaningful Work

Find meaning and purpose in your work. Connect with the broader impact of your contributions and seek out opportunities for growth and development. When work aligns with your values and passions, it becomes a source of fulfillment rather than a cause of burnout.

Disconnect and Recharge

Set boundaries around technology and create designated periods of rest and relaxation. Disconnect from work-related devices and activities during non-working hours to allow yourself time to recharge and rejuvenate. Prioritize activities that bring you joy and fulfillment outside of work.

Cultivate a Healthy Lifestyle

Maintain a healthy lifestyle that supports your well-being. Exercise regularly, eat nutritious meals, get enough sleep, and engage in activities that promote mental and physical health. A strong foundation of self-care can help protect you from burnout.

Seek Professional Support

If you're experiencing significant levels of stress or burnout, don't hesitate to seek professional help. A therapist or counselor can provide guidance, tools, and strategies for managing stress and building resilience. They can help you navigate the challenges and develop coping mechanisms to prevent burnout.

WORK-LIFE INTEGRATION

Finally, it's important to recognize the value of work-life

integration. Instead of striving for a perfect balance between work and personal life, seek integration and synergy between the two. Identify activities that bring you joy, fulfillment, and a sense of accomplishment in both domains. Foster a holistic approach to your life that allows for flexibility, adaptability, and the freedom to prioritize what matters most to you.

EMBRACING A BALANCED AND RESILIENT LIFE

Managing stress and preventing burnout is an ongoing process that requires self-awareness, intentionality, and self-care. By implementing the strategies discussed in this chapter and prioritizing your well-being, you can create a more balanced, fulfilling, and resilient life. Remember, your time and energy are precious resources, and it's crucial to protect and nurture them to make the most of your limited time. In the next chapter, we will explore the concept of lifelong learning and its role in personal and professional growth.

CHAPTER 20: LEARNING TO RELAX

I n our fast-paced and busy lives, the art of relaxation often takes a backseat. However, learning to relax is crucial for our overall well-being, productivity, and ability to make the most of our limited time. In this chapter, we will explore the importance of relaxation, the benefits it brings, and practical strategies for incorporating relaxation into our daily lives.

THE IMPORTANCE OF RELAXATION

Relaxation is the process of unwinding, letting go of tension, and allowing our bodies and minds to enter a state of calm and rejuvenation. It is an essential component of a balanced and fulfilling life. Here are some reasons why relaxation is important:

Stress Reduction

Relaxation serves as an antidote to stress. It helps to counteract the negative effects of chronic stress on our physical and mental health. By engaging in relaxation practices, we activate the body's relaxation response, which promotes a sense of calm, lowers stress hormones, and restores balance.

Improved Mental Well-being

Relaxation techniques, such as mindfulness and meditation, have been shown to reduce anxiety, depression, and improve overall mental well-being. Taking time to relax allows our minds to rest, recharge, and gain clarity, leading to improved focus, concentration, and problem-solving abilities.

Enhanced Productivity

Contrary to popular belief, relaxation doesn't hinder productivity; it actually enhances it. When we take regular breaks and engage in relaxation activities, we recharge our energy reserves, improve our cognitive function, and increase our ability to sustain focus and productivity over extended periods.

Physical Health Benefits

Relaxation has numerous physical health benefits. It helps to lower blood pressure, improve cardiovascular health, boost the immune system, and reduce the risk of stress-related illnesses. Regular relaxation practices also support better sleep, digestion, and overall bodily functioning.

Enhanced Creativity and Problem-solving

Relaxation fosters a state of mental and emotional openness that is conducive to creativity and innovative thinking. When we relax, we allow our minds to wander, make connections, and generate new ideas. Additionally, relaxation helps us approach problem-solving with a calm and clear mindset, enabling us to find more effective solutions.

Improved Relationships

When we are relaxed, we are more present and attentive in our interactions with others. By taking time to relax, we reduce irritability, stress, and emotional reactivity, enabling us to cultivate healthier and more meaningful relationships.

TYPES OF RELAXATION TECHNIQUES

There are numerous relaxation techniques that can help us unwind, reduce stress, and promote a sense of well-being. Here are some popular relaxation techniques to consider:

Mindfulness and Meditation

Mindfulness involves bringing non-judgmental awareness to the present moment. By focusing on our breath, sensations, or thoughts without judgment, we cultivate a sense of calm and deepen our connection with the present. Meditation practices, such as guided meditation or loving-kindness meditation, can also promote relaxation and inner peace.

Deep Breathing Exercises

Deep breathing exercises involve taking slow, deep breaths, focusing on the inhalation and exhalation. This practice activates the body's relaxation response, slows down the heart rate, and calms the mind. Techniques such as diaphragmatic breathing or alternate nostril breathing can be particularly effective in inducing relaxation.

Progressive Muscle Relaxation

Progressive muscle relaxation involves systematically tensing and then releasing each muscle group in the body. This technique helps to release physical tension and promote deep relaxation. By consciously relaxing our muscles, we also signal to our minds that it's time to unwind and let go of stress.

Yoga and Stretching

Yoga combines physical postures, breathing techniques, and mindfulness to promote relaxation and flexibility. Regular yoga practice can help release tension, increase body awareness, and improve overall well-being. Similarly, engaging in stretching exercises can relieve muscle stiffness and promote relaxation.

Visualization and Guided Imagery

Visualization involves creating mental images of peaceful or calming scenes, such as a beach or a tranquil forest. Guided imagery involves listening to recorded instructions that lead you through a calming visualization process. These techniques engage your senses and imagination to promote relaxation and reduce stress.

Engaging in Hobbies and Creative Activities

Engaging in activities you enjoy and find fulfilling can be highly relaxing. Whether it's painting, playing a musical instrument, gardening, or writing in a journal, immersing yourself in creative pursuits helps to shift your focus, bring joy, and foster a sense of relaxation.

Nature and Outdoor Time

Spending time in nature and connecting with the natural environment can have a profound impact on relaxation. Whether it's taking a walk in a park, going for a hike, or simply sitting in a garden, being in nature allows us to disconnect from the demands of daily life, find solace, and rejuvenate our senses.

Digital Detox

In our digitally connected world, constant exposure to screens and notifications can contribute to stress and overwhelm. Taking regular breaks from technology, whether it's a designated "digital detox" day or simply creating screen-free periods in your daily routine, can help to reduce mental clutter, increase focus, and promote relaxation.

STRATEGIES FOR INCORPORATING RELAXATION INTO DAILY LIFE

Incorporating relaxation into our daily lives requires intentional effort and commitment. Here are some strategies for integrating relaxation practices into your routine:

Prioritize Self-Care

Make self-care a non-negotiable part of your routine. Recognize that relaxation is not a luxury but a necessity for your well-being. Prioritize activities that promote relaxation, whether it's scheduling regular self-care time, booking a massage, or engaging in a hobby you enjoy.

Create a Relaxation Ritual

Establish a relaxation ritual that signals to your mind and body that it's time to unwind. This can be a specific routine or sequence of activities that you engage in before bed, during breaks, or at the end of the workday. It may include deep breathing, meditation, or engaging in a calming activity that you find soothing.

Schedule Relaxation Time

Allocate dedicated time for relaxation in your daily schedule. Treat relaxation as an important appointment and honor that commitment to yourself. Whether it's a short break during the day or an extended period in the evening, set aside time for relaxation and make it a non-negotiable part of your routine.

Practice Mindful Transitions

Incorporate moments of mindfulness and relaxation during transitions throughout your day. Use the time between tasks, meetings, or activities to pause, take a few deep breaths, and bring your attention to the present moment. This practice helps to reset your focus, release tension, and maintain a sense of calm amidst the busyness.

Set Boundaries

Set boundaries around your relaxation time. Communicate your needs and limitations to others and be assertive in protecting that time. Avoid over-committing or sacrificing your relaxation time for the sake of pleasing others. Remember that self-care is essential for your well-being and productivity.

Practice Gratitude

Cultivate a gratitude practice as a form of relaxation. Take a few moments each day to reflect on the things you're grateful for.

This practice helps to shift your focus from stressors to positive aspects of your life, fostering a sense of relaxation, contentment, and perspective.

Create a Relaxing Environment

Create a physical environment that supports relaxation. Declutter your space, incorporate soothing colors, and add elements such as soft lighting, plants, or calming scents. Designate a specific area in your home or workspace for relaxation, where you can retreat to when you need a moment of tranquility.

Be Present and Mindful

Practice being fully present and mindful in each moment. Engage in activities with full awareness and immerse yourself in the present experience. Whether it's enjoying a cup of tea, taking a walk, or engaging in a conversation, gives your full attention to the present moment, savoring the experience and cultivating relaxation.

OVERCOMING BARRIERS TO RELAXATION

Incorporating relaxation into our lives can face certain challenges. Here are strategies for overcoming common barriers:

Letting Go of Guilt

Let go of any guilt or self-judgment associated with relaxation. Recognize that taking time for yourself is not selfish but essential for your well-being. Embrace relaxation as a valuable investment in yourself that ultimately benefits your productivity, relationships, and overall quality of life.

Cultivating Consistency

Consistency is the key to reaping the benefits of relaxation. Aim to incorporate relaxation practices into your daily routine consistently, even if it's for a short period. Consistency builds the habit and reinforces the positive impact of relaxation on your well-being.

Adapting to Individual Preferences

Explore various relaxation techniques and find what resonates with you. Not all techniques will appeal to everyone, so experiment and discover what brings you the most relaxation and joy. Customize your relaxation practices to align with your preferences, interests, and values.

Overcoming Time Constraints

When time feels limited, remember that even a few minutes of relaxation can make a difference. Start small and gradually increase the duration as you prioritize relaxation. Look for pockets of time throughout your day that can be dedicated to relaxation, such as during breaks or before bedtime.

Practicing Self-Discipline

Develop self-discipline in prioritizing relaxation. Commit to making relaxation a priority and hold yourself accountable to incorporate it into your daily routine. Remind yourself of the benefits and the positive impact relaxation has on your overall well-being.

EMBRACING A RELAXATION MINDSET

Learning to relax is an ongoing journey that requires intentionality and self-awareness. By embracing relaxation as an integral part of your life, you can cultivate a sense of calm, improve your well-being, and make the most of your limited time. Remember, relaxation is not a luxury; it's a necessity for living a balanced, fulfilling, and meaningful life. In the next chapter, we will explore the concept of finding joy in everyday life and how it can enhance our well-being.

CHAPTER 21: FLEXIBILITY AND ADAPTABILITY

I n today's rapidly changing world, the ability to be flexible and adaptable is crucial for navigating the challenges and opportunities that come our way. Flexibility allows us to adjust our plans and approaches, while adaptability enables us to thrive in new and evolving circumstances. In this chapter, we will explore the importance of flexibility and adaptability, the benefits they bring, and strategies for cultivating these essential skills in our lives.

THE VALUE OF FLEXIBILITY AND ADAPTABILITY

Flexibility and adaptability are key qualities that enable us to navigate uncertainty, embrace change, and make the most of our limited time. Here are some reasons why these qualities are valuable:

Navigating Change

Change is inevitable in both personal and professional realms. Being flexible and adaptable allows us to navigate change with greater ease and resilience. Instead of resisting or fearing change, we can approach it with a growth mindset and view it as an opportunity for growth and learning.

Embracing New Opportunities

Flexibility and adaptability open doors to new opportunities. When we are open to trying new things, exploring different paths, and stepping outside our comfort zones, we increase our chances of discovering new passions, developing new skills, and achieving success in unexpected ways.

Problem-Solving and Innovation

Flexibility and adaptability enhance our problem-solving and innovative thinking abilities. When faced with challenges or setbacks, we can quickly assess the situation, generate creative solutions, and adapt our approach as needed. This enables us to overcome obstacles and find new ways of achieving our goals.

Enhancing Relationships

Flexibility and adaptability contribute to healthier and more fulfilling relationships. By being open to different perspectives, willing to compromise, and adjusting our communication styles to meet the needs of others, we build stronger connections and foster harmonious interactions.

Promoting Resilience and Well-being

Flexibility and adaptability are closely linked to resilience and well-being. When we can adapt to changing circumstances, we reduce stress, increase our ability to cope with challenges, and maintain a sense of balance and equilibrium. This, in turn, supports our overall mental and emotional well-being.

STRATEGIES FOR CULTIVATING FLEXIBILITY

Flexibility is the ability to adjust our plans, approaches, and mindset in response to changing circumstances. Here are strategies for cultivating flexibility in our lives:

Embrace Open-Mindedness

Cultivate an open mind and a willingness to consider different perspectives and ideas. Challenge your assumptions and preconceived notions, and be open to alternative approaches. This open-mindedness allows you to adapt your thinking and be receptive to new possibilities.

Practice Letting Go of Control

Recognize that not everything is within your control. Embrace the idea that change is inevitable and that you can't control every outcome. Instead of resisting or trying to control every detail, focus on what you can control—your attitude, actions, and responses.

Be Agile in Your Thinking

Develop agility in your thinking by being able to quickly shift perspectives and adapt to new information. Train yourself to be comfortable with ambiguity and uncertainty. This agility allows you to respond more effectively to unexpected challenges and changes.

Seek Opportunities for Growth

Embrace opportunities for personal and professional growth. Seek out experiences that challenge you, expose you to new ideas, or require you to step outside your comfort zone. By continually seeking growth, you develop the ability to adapt to new situations and embrace change more readily.

Learn from Mistakes and Setbacks

View mistakes and setbacks as learning opportunities rather than failures. Embrace a growth mindset that recognizes that setbacks are stepping stones to success. Reflect on what you can learn from these experiences and use that knowledge to inform your future actions and decisions.

Practice Resilience

Build resilience by developing coping mechanisms and strategies to bounce back from setbacks. Cultivate a positive mindset, nurture your physical and mental well-being, and seek support when needed. Resilience helps you adapt to challenges, maintain a sense of balance, and bounce back stronger.

Embrace Change as an Opportunity

Shift your perspective on change. Instead of seeing it as a disruption or a threat, view it as an opportunity for growth and transformation. Embrace change as a chance to learn, explore new possibilities, and expand your horizons.

Foster a Growth Mindset

Develop a growth mindset that embraces continuous learning and improvement. Believe that your abilities and intelligence can be developed through effort, practice, and resilience. This mindset allows you to adapt to new situations, learn new skills, and overcome challenges.

STRATEGIES FOR CULTIVATING ADAPTABILITY

Adaptability is the ability to adjust and thrive in new or changing circumstances. Here are strategies for cultivating adaptability in our lives:

Cultivate Self-Awareness

Develop self-awareness to understand your strengths, weaknesses, and areas for growth. Recognize your comfort zones and identify areas where you may be resistant to change. By understanding yourself, you can consciously work on expanding your comfort zones and embracing new experiences.

Develop a Growth Mindset

Adopt a growth mindset that believes in the potential for growth and development. See challenges as opportunities to learn and develop new skills. Embrace a positive attitude towards change and view it as a chance to expand your capabilities.

Embrace a Learning Orientation

Cultivate a learning orientation in all aspects of your life. Seek out new knowledge, develop new skills, and continuously seek opportunities for growth. Embrace a curiosity-driven mindset and approach new experiences with a desire to learn and adapt.

Practice Resilience and Self-Reflection

Develop resilience and self-reflection skills to navigate changes effectively. When faced with challenges or setbacks, take time to reflect on the situation, identify lessons learned, and adapt your approach. Cultivate a mindset that sees setbacks as temporary and uses them as stepping stones for growth.

Develop Interpersonal Skills

Build strong interpersonal skills to navigate changes and work effectively with others. Develop effective communication, collaboration, and problem-solving abilities. These skills enable you to adapt to different working styles, build positive relationships, and navigate conflicts constructively.

Embrace Continuous Learning

Commit to lifelong learning and professional development. Stay updated with industry trends, technological advancements, and new knowledge relevant to your field. Embracing continuous learning equips you with the skills and knowledge needed to adapt to evolving circumstances.

Cultivate Emotional Intelligence

Develop emotional intelligence to navigate change and adapt to different social and emotional contexts. Understand and manage your emotions effectively, empathize with others, and navigate interpersonal dynamics with awareness and sensitivity.

Foster a Supportive Network

Surround yourself with a supportive network of individuals who embrace change and encourage personal growth. Seek out mentors, colleagues, or friends who can provide guidance, support, and different perspectives. Engage in networking activities that expose you to diverse experiences and ideas.

EMBRACING FLEXIBILITY AND ADAPTABILITY IN DAILY LIFE

To truly embrace flexibility and adaptability, it's important to incorporate these qualities into our daily lives. Here are practical ways to do so:

Embrace a Growth Mindset

Cultivate a growth mindset in your daily life. Embrace challenges, view setbacks as learning opportunities, and continuously seek growth and improvement.

Seek New Experiences

Actively seek out new experiences that push you outside your comfort zone. Take on new projects, try new activities, or explore new environments. Embrace the unfamiliar and be open to learning from these experiences.

Embrace Change as a Constant

Recognize that change is a constant in life. Instead of resisting or fearing it, embrace change as a natural part of personal and professional growth. Embrace the opportunities that come with change and use them to your advantage.

Be Agile in Your Plans

Be willing to adjust your plans and goals when necessary. Understand that circumstances may change, and the path to success may require adaptation. Stay flexible and agile in your approach, always ready to pivot when needed.

Practice Resilience

Develop resilience to bounce back from setbacks and challenges. Cultivate a positive mindset, practice self-care, and seek support when needed. Build your resilience muscles to navigate changes with greater ease and grace.

Foster a Supportive Environment

Surround yourself with a supportive network of individuals who value flexibility and adaptability. Seek out mentors, colleagues, or friends who inspire and encourage you to embrace change. Create an environment that fosters growth, learning, and adaptability.

Learn from Failure

View failure as a learning opportunity rather than a defeat. When things don't go as planned, take the time to reflect on the experience, identify lessons learned, and apply them to future endeavors. Failure can provide valuable insights and propel you towards future success.

Continuously Learn and Evolve

Commit to lifelong learning and personal development. Stay curious, seek new knowledge, and develop new skills. Be proactive in staying updated with industry trends and advancements. The more you invest in your own growth, the more adaptable and flexible you become.

EMBRACING THE POWER OF FLEXIBILITY AND ADAPTABILITY

Flexibility and adaptability are essential qualities that allow us to navigate change, embrace new opportunities, and make the most of our limited time. By cultivating flexibility and adaptability in our lives, we can respond to challenges with resilience, embrace new possibilities, and thrive in a constantly evolving world.

Remember, being flexible and adaptable doesn't mean compromising your values or losing sight of your goals. It means being willing to adjust, explore new approaches, and embrace change as a catalyst for growth. By valuing flexibility and adaptability, you can unlock your full potential and create a life of purpose, success, and fulfillment. In the next chapter, we will explore the concept of time management and practical strategies for optimizing our use of time.

CHAPTER 22: THE IMPACT OF TECHNOLOGY

I n today's digital age, technology has become an integral part of our lives, shaping the way we work, communicate, and navigate the world. While technology has brought numerous benefits and advancements, it has also introduced new challenges and complexities when it comes to managing our time effectively. In this chapter, we will explore the impact of technology on our lives, the advantages and disadvantages it brings, and strategies for harnessing technology to maximize our use of time.

THE ADVANTAGES OF TECHNOLOGY

Technology has revolutionized the way we live and work, offering a wide range of advantages and opportunities. Here are some of the key benefits of technology:

Increased Efficiency and Productivity

Technological advancements have streamlined processes, automated tasks and enhanced efficiency. With the help of tools, software, and digital platforms, we can accomplish tasks more quickly and effectively. This increased efficiency allows us to accomplish more in less time.

Global Connectivity and Communication

Technology has bridged geographical gaps, enabling us to connect and communicate with people around the world. Through the internet, social media, and various communication platforms, we can collaborate with others, exchange ideas, and build relationships regardless of physical distance.

Access to Information and Knowledge

The internet has made a vast amount of information and knowledge readily accessible. With just a few clicks, we can find answers to our questions, learn new skills, and stay updated with the latest news and developments. This access to information empowers us to make informed decisions and expand our knowledge base.

Remote Work and Flexibility

Technological advancements have facilitated the rise of remote work and flexible work arrangements. With the help of communication tools, project management software, and cloud-based platforms, we can work from anywhere and collaborate with colleagues across different time zones. This flexibility allows for better work-life integration and the ability to optimize our use of time.

Automation and Time-saving

Technology has automated repetitive tasks and processes, saving us time and freeing up mental space for more meaningful and creative work. Automated systems, such as email filters, scheduling tools, and project management software, help us streamline our workflows and focus on high-value activities.

Enhanced Connectivity and Convenience

Smart-phones, tablets, and wearable devices have made connectivity and convenience a seamless part of our lives. We can access information, communicate, and manage our tasks on the go, enabling us to stay connected and productive wherever we are.

THE DISADVANTAGES AND CHALLENGES OF TECHNOLOGY

While technology brings many advantages, it also poses certain disadvantages and challenges that impact our use of time. It's important to be aware of these drawbacks and find ways to mitigate their impact:

Information Overload

The abundance of information available through technology can lead to information overload. It can be overwhelming to sift through vast amounts of data and filter out what's relevant and valuable. This overload can consume our time and attention, making it challenging to focus on important tasks.

Distractions and Multitasking

Technology introduces numerous distractions that can pull us away from our priorities and hinder our productivity. Notifications, social media, and endless digital stimuli can lead to constant multitasking, which decreases efficiency and impairs our ability to concentrate on a single task.

Sedentary Lifestyle

Excessive use of technology can contribute to a sedentary lifestyle. Sitting for extended periods in front of screens can negatively impact our physical health, leading to issues such as poor posture, back pain, and decreased overall well-being. It's essential to incorporate physical activity and movement into our routines to counterbalance the sedentary nature of technology use.

Impersonal Communication

While technology enables communication across vast distances, it can also lead to a loss of personal connection. Online interactions may lack the depth, nuance, and human connection that come with face-to-face communication. It's important to find ways to maintain and nurture meaningful relationships in a digital world.

Perpetual Connectivity and Work-life Boundaries

Technology blurs the boundaries between work and personal life. With constant access to work-related tools and communication, it can be challenging to disconnect and establish clear boundaries. This can lead to an "always-on" mentality, where work encroaches on personal time, leading to stress, burnout, and decreased overall well-being.

Privacy and Security Concerns

The digitization of personal information raises concerns about privacy and security. With the increasing prevalence of data breaches and cyber threats, it's important to be mindful of protecting our personal information and maintaining cyber security practices. Addressing these concerns can require additional time and attention.

STRATEGIES FOR HARNESSING TECHNOLOGY FOR EFFECTIVE TIME MANAGEMENT

While technology poses challenges, it also offers immense potential for optimizing our use of time. Here are strategies for harnessing technology to maximize our productivity and well-being:

Set Digital Boundaries

Establish clear boundaries around your technology use. Designate specific times for checking emails, social media, or engaging in online activities. Use tools and features such as "Do Not Disturb" mode or app blockers to minimize distractions and maintain focus during dedicated work periods.

Practice Digital Detox

Regularly disconnect from technology to give yourself a break and recharge. Designate periods of time, whether it's a few hours or a full day, to unplug and engage in offline activities that bring you joy and relaxation. Use this time to rejuvenate your mind and foster a healthier relationship with technology.

Optimize Digital Tools

Identify and utilize digital tools that enhance your productivity and organization. Explore task management apps, note-taking tools, or time-tracking software that aligns with your needs and preferences. Streamline your workflows by leveraging technology to automate repetitive tasks and reduce manual effort.

Practice Mindful Technology Use

Be intentional and mindful when using technology. Before engaging with digital devices, pause and ask yourself if the activity aligns with your goals and priorities. Set specific intentions for your technology use, ensuring it serves a purpose rather than becoming a source of mindless distraction.

Curate Your Digital Environment

Take control of your digital environment by curating it to support your well-being and productivity. Declutter your digital spaces, organize files and folders, and unsubscribe from unnecessary emails and subscriptions. Optimize your digital workspace to minimize visual distractions and create a clutter-free environment.

Use Technology for Learning and Growth

Leverage technology for continuous learning and personal growth. Access online courses, educational platforms, or podcasts to expand your knowledge and develop new skills.

Set aside dedicated time for intentional learning and utilize technology as a tool for self-improvement.

Cultivate Digital Wellness Practices

Develop digital wellness practices to promote a healthy relationship with technology. Take regular breaks to stretch and move your body. Practice mindful breathing or meditation exercises to counteract the sedentary nature of technology use. Be mindful of your posture and incorporate ergonomic setups to support physical well-being.

Prioritize Face-to-face Interactions

While technology offers convenience, make an effort to prioritize face-to-face interactions when possible. Schedule in-person meetings, engage in social activities, and nurture meaningful relationships offline. Foster a balanced approach that integrates technology as a facilitator rather than a replacement for human connection.

EMBRACING A HEALTHY RELATIONSHIP WITH TECHNOLOGY

To effectively manage our time in the digital age, it's crucial to cultivate a healthy relationship with technology. By understanding the advantages and disadvantages of technology and implementing strategies for intentional and mindful use, we can harness its potential while mitigating its drawbacks. Embrace technology as a tool to support your goals, productivity, and overall well-being, ensuring that it enhances rather than hinders your ability to value your time.

In the next chapter, we will explore the concept of self-reflection and how it can help us gain clarity, make informed decisions, and align our actions with our values and goals.

CHAPTER 23: CONTINUOUS IMPROVEMENT

I n the pursuit of making the most of our limited time, it is essential to adopt a mindset of continuous improvement. Continuous improvement involves a commitment to ongoing learning, growth, and refinement of our skills, habits, and processes. In this chapter, we will explore the importance of continuous improvement, the benefits it brings, and practical strategies for incorporating it into our lives.

THE POWER OF CONTINUOUS IMPROVEMENT

Continuous improvement is a philosophy and approach that acknowledges the need for constant learning and growth. It is rooted in the belief that there is always room for improvement and that small, incremental changes over time can lead to significant progress. Here are some reasons why continuous improvement is valuable:

Personal Growth and Development

Continuous improvement allows us to continuously expand our knowledge, skills, and abilities. It enables us to stay relevant in a rapidly changing world and adapt to new challenges and opportunities. By committing to lifelong learning, we nurture personal growth and development, enhancing our capabilities and unlocking our full potential.

Adaptability and Resilience

In a dynamic and ever-changing environment, adaptability and resilience are crucial. Continuous improvement fosters these qualities by instilling a growth mindset and an openness to change. It enables us to embrace new ideas, perspectives, and technologies, and respond effectively to shifting circumstances.

Enhanced Productivity and Efficiency

Continuous improvement helps us identify inefficiencies, streamline processes, and eliminate wasteful practices. By consistently evaluating and refining our approaches, we can optimize our use of time and resources, enhancing our productivity and efficiency. This leads to better outcomes and enables us to accomplish more in less time.

Innovation and Creativity

Continuous improvement encourages us to challenge the status quo and think innovatively. By seeking new solutions, exploring alternative approaches, and embracing a spirit of curiosity, we foster creativity and generate fresh ideas. This innovative thinking allows us to find novel ways of approaching tasks, solving problems, and creating value.

Quality and Excellence

Continuous improvement fosters a commitment to quality and excellence in everything we do. By consistently seeking ways to improve, we raise our standards, deliver better results, and exceed expectations. This dedication to excellence not only benefits our own work but also contributes to the success and reputation of our endeavors.

Self-Reflection and Self-Awareness

Continuous improvement requires self-reflection and self-awareness. It encourages us to regularly evaluate our actions, behaviors, and outcomes, and identify areas for growth. By developing this introspective habit, we gain clarity about our strengths, weaknesses, and areas that need improvement, enabling us to make more informed decisions and take purposeful action.

STRATEGIES FOR CONTINUOUS IMPROVEMENT

To embrace continuous improvement in our lives, we can adopt various strategies and practices. Here are some practical approaches to incorporate continuous improvement:

Set Clear Goals

Establish clear and specific goals that align with your vision and values. Clearly defined goals provide a sense of direction and purpose, serving as a reference point for continuous improvement efforts. Break down larger goals into smaller, manageable milestones to track progress and celebrate achievements along the way.

Embrace a Growth Mindset

Adopt a growth mindset that views challenges, failures, and setbacks as opportunities for learning and growth. Embrace a belief that abilities and intelligence can be developed through effort, practice, and resilience. Cultivate a positive attitude towards mistakes and see them as stepping stones towards improvement.

Cultivate a Learning Mindset

Nurture a thirst for knowledge and continuous learning. Embrace a mindset that recognizes that learning is a lifelong journey. Seek out opportunities for growth, such as attending workshops, reading books, taking courses, or participating in online learning platforms. Actively seek feedback from others to gain different perspectives and insights.

Practice Reflection and Self-Evaluation

Set aside dedicated time for reflection and self-evaluation. Regularly assess your progress, actions, and outcomes. Identify areas where you can improve and develop action plans to address them. Reflect on both successes and failures to extract lessons learned and identify opportunities for growth.

Embrace Kaizen Principles

Kaizen, a Japanese term for continuous improvement, emphasizes making small, incremental changes over time. Embrace this philosophy by seeking opportunities for small improvements in your daily routines, workflows, and habits. Look for ways to refine processes, eliminate waste, and enhance efficiency.

Seek Feedback and Learn from Others

Actively seek feedback from mentors, colleagues, or trusted individuals in your field. Be open to constructive criticism and different perspectives. Engage in discussions, collaborative projects, and peer learning opportunities to gain insights and broaden your knowledge.

Experiment and Embrace Failure

Be willing to experiment and take calculated risks. Embrace failure as a natural part of the learning process. Encourage a culture of experimentation and innovation, both in your personal and professional life. Celebrate the lessons learned from failures and use them to iterate and improve.

Develop Action Plans

Translate your insights and goals into actionable steps. Break down larger goals into smaller, manageable tasks. Create action plans that outline specific actions, timelines, and milestones. Regularly review and adjust your plans as needed, ensuring they align with your continuous improvement objectives.

INTEGRATING CONTINUOUS

IMPROVEMENT INTO DAILY LIFE

To fully embrace continuous improvement, it is important to integrate it into your daily life. Here are practical ways to incorporate continuous improvement into your routines:

Daily Reflection

Set aside time each day for reflection. Review your accomplishments, challenges, and areas for improvement. Identify lessons learned and opportunities for growth. Use this reflection time to celebrate successes, recalibrate your actions, and plan for the next steps.

Skill Development

Continuously develop your skills and knowledge in your area of expertise. Stay updated with industry trends, advancements, and best practices. Seek out professional development opportunities, whether it's attending workshops, webinars, or conferences. Invest in courses or certifications that enhance your skill set.

Peer Learning and Collaboration

Engage in peer learning and collaborative projects. Seek opportunities to share knowledge and expertise with others. Participate in communities or professional networks where you can exchange ideas and learn from others. Collaborate on projects that expose you to different perspectives and approaches.

Performance Reviews

Conduct regular performance reviews of your work or projects. Evaluate your progress, outcomes, and areas for improvement. Seek feedback from supervisors, mentors, or colleagues. Use this feedback to inform your continuous improvement efforts and set new goals.

Time Management Review

Regularly review your time management practices and identify areas for improvement. Assess how effectively you are allocating your time, identify time-wasting activities, and seek opportunities for better prioritization and organization. Adjust your routines and habits to optimize your use of time.

Continuous Learning Environment

Create an environment that fosters continuous learning. Surround yourself with individuals who value personal growth and improvement. Engage in conversations that stimulate learning and exchange of ideas. Develop habits such as reading, listening to podcasts, or engaging in thought-provoking discussions that expand your knowledge.

Celebrate Progress

Acknowledge and celebrate your progress and achievements along the journey of continuous improvement. Take time to appreciate the milestones you have reached and the growth you have experienced. Celebrate not only the big successes but also the small wins that contribute to your overall improvement.

THE JOURNEY OF CONTINUOUS IMPROVEMENT

Embracing continuous improvement is a lifelong journey. It requires a commitment to personal growth, a willingness to learn, and a dedication to refining our skills and habits. By adopting a growth mindset, regularly reflecting on our actions, and seeking opportunities for improvement, we can make significant strides in optimizing our use of time and maximizing our potential.

Remember, continuous improvement is not about perfection or reaching an end destination. It is a process of constant evolution, growth, and refinement. Embrace the journey and the transformative power it holds. In the next chapter, we will explore the importance of self-care and its role in maintaining a

balanced and fulfilling life.

CHAPTER 24: TEACHING TIME MANAGEMENT SKILLS

Time management is a vital skill that plays a crucial role in our personal and professional lives. Teaching effective time management skills equips individuals with the tools and techniques needed to prioritize tasks, make the most of their limited time, and achieve their goals. In this chapter, we will explore the importance of teaching time management skills, strategies for effective instruction, and practical tips for helping others develop strong time management habits.

THE IMPORTANCE OF TEACHING TIME MANAGEMENT SKILLS

Time management skills are not innate; they are learned and honed over time. By teaching time management skills, we empower individuals to take control of their time and enhance their productivity. Here are some reasons why teaching time management skills is important:

Improved Productivity and Efficiency

Effective time management techniques enable individuals to optimize their use of time, allowing them to accomplish more tasks in less time. By learning how to prioritize, plan, and manage their workload effectively, individuals can increase their productivity and efficiency.

Reduced Stress and Overwhelm

Time management skills help individuals avoid the feeling of being overwhelmed by tasks and deadlines. By learning how to manage their time effectively, individuals can reduce stress levels and experience a greater sense of control and calmness in their lives.

Goal Achievement

Time management skills are instrumental in helping individuals set and achieve their goals. By learning how to allocate time wisely and focus on the most important tasks, individuals can make progress towards their objectives and experience a sense of accomplishment.

Work-Life Balance

Effective time management enables individuals to strike a balance between their personal and professional lives. By learning how to allocate time for both work and personal activities, individuals can experience greater satisfaction and harmony in their lives.

Skill Development

Teaching time management skills provides individuals with a valuable life skill that can benefit them in various contexts. Time management skills foster discipline, organization, and self-motivation, which are transferable skills that can be applied to different areas of life.

STRATEGIES FOR EFFECTIVE INSTRUCTION

When teaching time management skills, it is important to employ strategies that engage learners and facilitate their understanding and application of the concepts. Here are some strategies for effective instruction:

Tailor Instruction to Individual Needs

Recognize that individuals have different learning styles and preferences. Adapt your teaching approach to accommodate diverse learning styles, whether it be visual, auditory, or kinesthetic. Provide a variety of instructional materials, such as written guides, videos, or interactive activities, to cater to different learning preferences.

Set Clear Learning Objectives

Clearly communicate the learning objectives to the learners. Clearly define what they will be able to do or achieve as a result of the instruction. This clarity helps learners understand the purpose of the lesson and what they are expected to gain from it.

Provide Practical Examples and Case Studies

Use real-life examples and case studies to illustrate the application of time management skills. Show how effective time management can positively impact productivity, goal achievement, and work-life balance. Encourage learners to relate the examples to their own lives and reflect on how they can apply the principles in their unique situations.

Encourage Active Participation

Engage learners actively in the learning process. Encourage participation through group discussions, role-playing activities, or hands-on exercises. This active involvement helps learners internalize the concepts and apply them to their own lives.

Foster a Supportive Learning Environment

Create a supportive and non-judgmental learning environment. Encourage open dialogue, questions, and discussions. Provide constructive feedback and guidance to help learners improve their time management skills. Foster a sense of collaboration and mutual support among learners, allowing them to learn from each other's experiences and perspectives.

Break Down Complex Concepts

Break down complex time management concepts into manageable, bite-sized pieces. Present the information in a clear and organized manner, using simple language and visual aids to enhance understanding. Provide step-by-step instructions and clear guidelines to help learners implement the concepts effectively.

Offer Ongoing Support and Guidance

Recognize that time management is an ongoing process. Offer ongoing support and guidance to learners as they implement the skills in their daily lives. Provide resources, such as checklists, templates, or online tools, that learners can use to reinforce their learning and continue their growth beyond the instructional period.

PRACTICAL TIPS FOR TEACHING TIME MANAGEMENT SKILLS

When teaching time management skills, it can be helpful to incorporate practical tips and strategies that learners can immediately apply in their lives. Here are some practical tips for teaching time management skills:

Prioritization Techniques

Introduce various techniques for prioritizing tasks, such as the Eisenhower Matrix or the ABC method. Teach learners how to identify high-priority tasks, delegate or eliminate non-essential tasks, and allocate time and resources based on importance and urgency.

Time Blocking

Teach learners the concept of time blocking, where they allocate specific time blocks for different tasks or activities. Demonstrate how to create a schedule that accounts for both work and personal commitments, ensuring that important tasks receive dedicated time and attention.

Goal Setting Strategies

Guide learners in setting SMART (Specific, Measurable, Achievable, Relevant, Time-bound) goals. Teach them how to break down long-term goals into smaller, manageable milestones and develop action plans to achieve them. Emphasize the importance of regularly reviewing and adjusting goals as circumstances change.

Proactive Planning

Encourage learners to adopt proactive planning habits. Teach them the importance of scheduling regular planning sessions to review upcoming tasks, deadlines, and commitments. Help them develop techniques for effective task organization, such as using to-do lists, digital task managers, or project management tools.

Time Tracking and Analysis

Introduce the practice of time tracking and analysis. Teach learners how to record and analyze their time usage to identify patterns, time wasters, and areas for improvement. Help them understand how their time is currently being allocated and guide them in making adjustments to optimize their productivity.

Stress Management Techniques

Incorporate stress management techniques into the instruction. Teach learners how to recognize and manage stress effectively. Introduce strategies such as mindfulness, deep breathing exercises, or physical activities that can help individuals reduce stress levels and maintain focus and productivity.

Effective Communication Skills

Highlight the importance of effective communication in time management. Teach learners how to communicate their time constraints, set boundaries, and delegate tasks effectively. Help them develop skills in assertive communication, active listening, and negotiation to enhance their interactions with others.

Continuous Improvement Mindset

Encourage a mindset of continuous improvement in learners. Emphasize that time management skills are not static but require ongoing refinement and adjustment. Teach them strategies for self-reflection, self-evaluation, and learning from their experiences to continually enhance their time management practices.

TEACHING TIME MANAGEMENT TO DIFFERENT AUDIENCES

When teaching time management skills, it is important to consider the specific needs and contexts of your audience. Time management skills are relevant to individuals of all ages and backgrounds. Here are some considerations for teaching time management to different audiences:

Students and Young Learners

Teach time management skills to students early on to equip them with valuable skills for academic success. Focus on practical techniques such as task prioritization, effective study habits, and time allocation for extracurricular activities. Incorporate interactive activities and games to make the learning experience engaging and enjoyable.

Professionals and Employees

Tailor time management instruction to the specific challenges faced by professionals and employees. Address topics such as managing workloads, setting boundaries, and balancing competing priorities. Discuss techniques for managing email overload, conducting effective meetings, and managing interruptions in the workplace.

Entrepreneurs and Business Owners

Provide time management strategies tailored to the unique demands of entrepreneurs and business owners. Cover topics such as prioritizing business tasks, delegating responsibilities, and maintaining a healthy work-life balance. Address the challenges of managing multiple projects, handling uncertainty, and effectively utilizing resources.

Parents and Caregivers

Teach time management skills to parents and caregivers to help them juggle multiple responsibilities. Focus on techniques for managing household tasks, family schedules, and personal time. Discuss strategies for setting boundaries, fostering effective communication, and practicing self-care in the midst of parenting and care giving responsibilities.

SUPPORTING CONTINUED GROWTH AND DEVELOPMENT

Teaching time management skills is not a one-time event; it is an ongoing process. Provide learners with resources and support beyond the instructional period to ensure their continued growth and development. Offer follow-up sessions, newsletters, or online communities where learners can seek guidance, share experiences, and continue their learning journey.

By teaching effective time management skills, we empower individuals to take control of their time, enhance their productivity, and lead more balanced and fulfilling lives. Encourage learners to embrace a lifelong commitment to continuous improvement in their time management practices. In the next chapter, we will explore the concept of work-life integration and strategies for finding harmony between work and personal life commitments.

CHAPTER 25: CONCLUSION

I n this journey of exploring the importance of valuing our time, we have delved into various aspects of time management, productivity, and personal growth. We have recognized that time is a finite resource, and how we choose to use it greatly impacts the quality of our lives and our ability to achieve our goals. Throughout this book, "It's Limited: Value Your Time," we have explored strategies, techniques, and principles to help us make the most of the time we have.

In this concluding chapter, we will summarize the key lessons learned and reiterate the importance of valuing our time. We will also reflect on the transformational impact that effective time management can have on our personal and professional lives.

RECAP OF KEY LESSONS

Throughout this book, we have covered a wide range of topics related to time management, productivity, and personal growth. Here is a recap of some of the key lessons learned:

Time is a Precious Resource

Time is a limited resource that cannot be replenished. Understanding the value of time and recognizing that it is our most precious asset is the first step towards effective time management.

Mindset Matters

Adopting a growth mindset and cultivating a positive attitude towards time management is essential. Embrace the belief that you have the power to take control of your time and make meaningful choices.

Setting Clear Priorities

Setting clear priorities is fundamental to effective time management. Identify your most important tasks and align your actions with your long-term goals and values.

Goal Setting and Planning

Goal setting and planning provide a roadmap for success. Break down your goals into actionable steps, create realistic timelines, and regularly review and adjust your plans as needed.

Overcoming Procrastination

Procrastination is a common obstacle to effective time management. Learn strategies to overcome procrastination, such as breaking tasks into smaller parts, utilizing time-blocking techniques, and leveraging accountability.

Managing Distractions

In today's digital age, managing distractions is crucial. Create an environment conducive to focus by minimizing distractions, practicing mindful technology use, and implementing strategies to reduce interruptions.

Effective Communication

Effective communication is key to managing time and fostering productive relationships. Learn to communicate assertively, set boundaries, and delegate tasks effectively.

Work-Life Integration

Striving for work-life integration, rather than work-life balance, enables us to harmonize our personal and professional lives. Recognize the importance of self-care, establish boundaries, and cultivate a supportive network.

Continuous Improvement

Embrace a mindset of continuous improvement. Regularly evaluate your time management practices, seek opportunities for growth, and adopt strategies for lifelong learning.

THE TRANSFORMATIONAL POWER OF EFFECTIVE TIME MANAGEMENT

By implementing the principles and strategies outlined in this book, you have the potential to experience a transformational shift in your life. Effective time management can lead to numerous benefits:

Increased Productivity

Efficiently managing your time allows you to accomplish more in less time. By prioritizing tasks, eliminating distractions, and streamlining processes, you can boost your productivity and achieve your goals more effectively.

Improved Focus and Concentration

Time management techniques help improve your ability to focus and concentrate on the task at hand. By minimizing interruptions, practicing deep work, and utilizing techniques like time blocking, you can enhance your ability to stay focused and produce high-quality work.

Enhanced Well-being

Valuing your time and finding a balance between work and personal life contributes to your overall well-being. By allocating time for self-care, pursuing hobbies, and nurturing relationships, you can experience greater fulfillment, reduced stress levels, and improved mental and physical health.

Goal Attainment

Effective time management empowers you to set and achieve your goals. By aligning your actions with your long-term aspirations, breaking down goals into actionable steps, and consistently working towards them, you can make significant progress and realize your ambitions.

Increased Opportunities

By optimizing your use of time, you open yourself up to new opportunities. Effective time management allows you to create space for personal and professional growth, take on new challenges, and explore avenues that align with your passions and values.

EMBRACING A TIME-VALUING LIFESTYLE

To truly value your time, it is essential to adopt time-valuing habits and incorporate the principles of effective time management into your daily life. Here are some final reminders as you embark on your journey:

Mindfulness and Intentionality

Cultivate mindfulness and intentionality in how you use your time. Be present in each moment, consciously choose how you spend your time, and regularly evaluate whether your actions align with your priorities and values.

Flexibility and Adaptability

Recognize that life is fluid and circumstances may change. Embrace flexibility and adaptability in your time management practices. Be prepared to adjust your plans and approaches as needed while staying focused on your long-term goals.

Self-compassion and Resilience

Be kind to yourself and practice self-compassion. Recognize that time management is an ongoing journey and that setbacks and challenges are part of the process. Cultivate resilience to bounce back from setbacks and learn from your experiences.

Lifelong Learning

Embrace the mindset of a lifelong learner. Continually seek opportunities for growth, explore new strategies, and expand your knowledge and skills. Commit to continuous improvement and adapt to new trends and technologies that can enhance your time management practices.

FINAL THOUGHTS

As we conclude this book, "It's Limited: Value Your Time," remember that time is a precious resource that cannot be regained once it is gone. By valuing your time, adopting effective time management practices, and continually seeking growth and improvement, you have the power to shape your life, achieve your goals, and experience greater fulfillment.

Embrace the principles and strategies shared in this book, adapt them to your unique circumstances, and make a commitment to value your time. Embrace the opportunities that effective time management presents and create a life that is aligned with your passions, values, and aspirations.

As you move forward, remember that time is limited, but your potential is limitless. Value your time, value yourself, and embrace the incredible journey that lies ahead.

About The Author

Cregg Hampton

Cregg Hampton is a visionary thought leader, entrepreneur, and time management expert with a deep passion for personal development and helping individuals unlock their full potential. With a wealth of knowledge and experience in the field of time management, Cregg is a sought-after speaker, coach, and consultant, inspiring audiences worldwide to embrace the value of time and live more fulfilling lives.

As a young child, Cregg always had an innate curiosity about the nature of time and how it shapes human existence. He would spend hours contemplating the concept of time and its influence on our perceptions and decisions. This fascination only intensified as he grew older and encountered the relentless demands of school, work, and other responsibilities.

Cregg's journey into the world of time management began during his university years. As a driven and ambitious student, he found himself juggling academics, extracurricular activities, and social commitments, often feeling overwhelmed by the sheer volume of tasks before him. This sense of urgency ignited a passion within him to explore ways to optimize his time and productivity without sacrificing his well-being.

Driven by an insatiable thirst for knowledge, Cregg embarked on a relentless pursuit of understanding the mechanics of time management. He immersed himself in academic research, delving into psychology, neuroscience, and the philosophy of time. Additionally, he sought wisdom from ancient and modern thinkers, exploring the works of productivity gurus, philosophers, and spiritual leaders.

Cregg's dedication to learning and growth allowed him to develop a comprehensive and multidimensional approach to time management—one that extends beyond mere efficiency and encompasses a deeper appreciation for the present moment. His insights and strategies go beyond conventional productivity techniques, as he encourages readers and audiences to embrace mindfulness, intentionality, and purpose-driven living.

Recognizing the transformative power of effective time management, Cregg co-founded Time Mastery Academy—a platform dedicated to empowering individuals and organizations to optimize their time and achieve their goals. Through this venture, he has helped countless individuals from various backgrounds improve their time management skills, leading to increased productivity, well-being, and success.

As a keynote speaker and workshop facilitator, Cregg has shared his expertise with audiences at universities, corporate events, and conferences worldwide. His dynamic and engaging presentations resonate with diverse audiences, inspiring them to view time as a valuable resource and empowering them to make intentional choices that align with their aspirations.

In addition to his work in time management, Cregg is a successful entrepreneur and business strategist. He has founded and co-founded multiple ventures, including technology startups and social impact initiatives, driven by his desire to make a positive difference in the world.

Beyond his professional endeavors, Cregg is deeply committed to giving back to the community. He actively participates in philanthropic initiatives, supporting causes related to education, environmental conservation, and youth empowerment.

Cregg holds a Bachelor's degree in Business Administration from a prestigious university, where he excelled academically and demonstrated exceptional leadership skills. He continues to engage in lifelong learning, staying at the forefront of the latest research and trends in time management and personal development.

As a prolific writer, Cregg has contributed to various publications, sharing his insights on time management, productivity, and personal growth. "Value Your Time" marks his debut as an author, allowing him to share his comprehensive approach to time management with a global audience.

In "Value Your Time," Cregg draws upon his wealth of knowledge, experiences, and unique perspective to present a comprehensive guide to time management. His writing is characterized by its clarity, authenticity, and relatability, making complex concepts accessible to readers of all backgrounds and ages.

When he is not writing or working on his entrepreneurial ventures, Cregg enjoys spending time with family and friends, engaging in outdoor activities, and nurturing his love for photography and travel.

With "Value Your Time," Cregg Hampton invites readers on a transformative journey—one that will empower them to embrace the value of time, discover their true potential, and lead lives of intention, fulfillment, and purpose.

For more information about Cregg Hampton and his work, you can visit his website at www.cregghampton.com.

Connect with Cregg on social media:

Instagram: @cregghampton LinkedIn: linkedin.com/in/cregghampton Twitter: @cregghampton Facebook: facebook.com/cregghamptonofficial

Join the Time Mastery Academy community for exclusive content, resources, and updates:

Website: www.timemasteryacademy.com Instagram: @timemasteryacademy LinkedIn: linkedin.com/company/timemasteryacademy Twitter: @timemasteryacad Facebook: facebook.com/timemasteryacademy

We hope that "Value Your Time" serves as a guiding light on your journey towards embracing the value of time and creating a life of intention, joy, and fulfillment.

Praise For Author

"Value Your Time" is an extraordinary book that transcends the conventional boundaries of time management. Cregg Hampton's insights and wisdom are a breath of fresh air in a world that often prioritizes busyness over true productivity. This book is a powerful reminder that time is not a commodity to be hoarded but a precious resource to be cherished and utilized with purpose.
Deepak Chopra, New York Times bestselling author and spiritual leader

Cregg Hampton's approach to time management is nothing short of revolutionary. "Value Your Time" is a thought-provoking and deeply insightful guide to reclaiming control over our lives and embracing the true essence of time. This book is a must-read for anyone seeking to live a more meaningful and fulfilling life.
Gretchen Rubin, bestselling author of "The Happiness Project"

"Value Your Time" is a masterpiece that offers a comprehensive and holistic approach to time management. Cregg Hampton's writing is both eloquent and relatable, making complex concepts accessible to readers of all backgrounds. This book has the power to transform the way we view time and its impact on our lives.
Daniel H. Pink, bestselling author of "When: The Scientific Secrets of Perfect Timing"

As a business executive juggling multiple responsibilities, I have always struggled to find a balance between productivity and well-

being. "Value Your Time" has been a game-changer for me. Cregg Hampton's strategies and insights have helped me optimize my time and achieve more with less stress. This book is a must-read for anyone seeking to enhance their productivity and find harmony in their personal and professional lives.
Sheryl Sandberg, COO of Facebook and bestselling author of "Lean In"

Cregg Hampton's "Value Your Time" is a rare gem in the self-help genre. This book goes beyond the usual time management tips and delves into the deeper meaning of time and its impact on our lives. With compelling anecdotes, practical exercises, and timeless wisdom, Cregg offers a transformative approach to time management that can revolutionize how we live and work.
Simon Sinek, bestselling author of "Start with Why" and "The Infinite Game"

"Value Your Time" is a masterclass in time management and personal development. Cregg Hampton's passion for the subject shines through every page, and his writing is both inspiring and actionable. This book is a valuable resource for anyone seeking to optimize their time and create a life of purpose and fulfillment.
Marie Forleo, bestselling author and host of "MarieTV"

Cregg Hampton's "Value Your Time" is a book that will stay with you long after you've turned the last page. His profound insights and practical strategies have transformed the way I approach time management and productivity. This book is a game-changer for anyone seeking to unlock their full potential and make the most of every moment.
Arianna Huffington, founder of The Huffington Post and author of "Thrive"

As a productivity enthusiast, I have read countless books on time management, but "Value Your Time" stands out as a true masterpiece. Cregg Hampton's unique perspective on time and

productivity has revolutionized the way I approach my daily tasks and responsibilities. This book is a must-read for anyone seeking to make the most of their time and lead a more fulfilling life.
Brian Tracy, bestselling author of "Eat That Frog!" and productivity expert

"Value Your Time" is a brilliant and refreshing take on time management. Cregg Hampton's writing is engaging and relatable, making complex concepts accessible to readers of all backgrounds. This book is a game-changer for anyone seeking to optimize their time, improve their productivity, and lead a more balanced and meaningful life.
Cal Newport, bestselling author of "Deep Work" and "Digital Minimalism"

Cregg Hampton's "Value Your Time" is a profound and transformative guide to time management. His unique approach combines practical strategies with philosophical insights, making this book a rare gem in the genre. I highly recommend "Value Your Time" to anyone seeking to unlock their full potential and lead a life of purpose and fulfillment.
Tony Robbins, #1 New York Times bestselling author and life coach

In "Value Your Time," Cregg Hampton presents a holistic and empowering approach to time management. His insights and strategies have helped me optimize my time and achieve more with less stress. This book is a game-changer for anyone seeking to make the most of their time and lead a more fulfilling life.
Mel Robbins, bestselling author of "The 5 Second Rule" and motivational speaker

Cregg Hampton's "Value Your Time" is a transformative guide to time management and personal growth. His writing is both inspiring and practical, offering readers a wealth of insights and strategies to optimize their time and achieve their goals. This book is a valuable resource for anyone seeking to live a life of intention and fulfillment.

Jay Shetty, bestselling author of "Think Like a Monk" and motivational speaker

"Value Your Time" is a must-read for anyone seeking to unlock their full potential and embrace the true essence of time. Cregg Hampton's writing is both eloquent and relatable, making this book a valuable resource for readers of all backgrounds. I highly recommend "Value Your Time" to anyone seeking to optimize their time and lead a more fulfilling life.
Eckhart Tolle, bestselling author of "The Power of Now" and spiritual teacher

In "Value Your Time," Cregg Hampton presents a powerful and transformative approach to time management. His insights and strategies have helped me optimize my time and achieve more with less stress. This book is a game-changer for anyone seeking to make the most of their time and lead a more fulfilling life.
Brendon Burchard, #1 New York Times bestselling author and high-performance coach

Cregg Hampton's "Value Your Time" is a powerful and practical guide to time management. His unique approach combines practical strategies with philosophical insights, making this book a rare gem in the genre. I highly recommend "Value Your Time" to anyone seeking to optimize their time and lead a more balanced and meaningful life.
Hal Elrod, bestselling author of "The Miracle Morning" and motivational speaker

Epilogue

As we reach the end of "Value Your Time," I hope you have found this journey of exploration and transformation to be as enlightening and empowering as I have. We have delved into the essence of time and its profound impact on our lives, recognizing that time is not merely a commodity to be spent, but a valuable resource to be cherished and utilized with purpose.

Throughout this book, we have explored the importance of understanding our relationship with time, setting priorities, and embracing mindfulness in our daily lives. We have learned to overcome procrastination, avoid time-wasting activities, and develop effective planning techniques. We have discovered the power of delegation, the importance of saying no, and the significance of time blocking.

In "Value Your Time," we have also examined the impact of technology on our relationship with time and the need for continuous improvement in our time management practices. We have explored the importance of a healthy work-life balance, the benefits of relaxation, and the significance of flexibility and adaptability in our fast-paced world.

The journey through these pages has been one of self-discovery and growth, and I hope that the insights and strategies presented here have empowered you to make intentional choices and embrace a more fulfilling and purpose-driven life.

As you continue your journey beyond this book, I encourage you to remain committed to the principles of time management and personal growth. Remember that time is a finite and precious resource; it is limited and cannot be replenished. Therefore, how we choose to spend our time matters immensely.

Embrace mindfulness and time awareness as your guiding principles. Cultivate a deep appreciation for the present moment, and be fully engaged in each task you undertake. Learn to set clear priorities and focus on what truly matters. Say no to activities and commitments that do not align with your goals and values.

Efficiently manage distractions and avoid time-wasting habits. Embrace the power of habits to build a solid foundation for a productive and fulfilling life. Seek a healthy work-life balance, and learn to relax and recharge regularly.

Adaptability and flexibility are essential traits in a world that is constantly evolving. Embrace change with an open mind and a willingness to learn and grow. Continuous improvement is key to staying ahead in our dynamic world, and a commitment to lifelong learning will serve you well on your journey.

In the pursuit of time management, remember that there is no one-size-fits-all solution. Each individual's journey is unique, and it is essential to find strategies that resonate with your personality, goals, and circumstances. Be patient with yourself and embrace progress, not perfection.

As you implement the principles of time management in your life, I encourage you to share this knowledge with others. Teach time management skills to your family, friends, colleagues, and community. Empower others to value their time and lead more fulfilling lives.

Finally, I want to express my deepest gratitude to you, the reader. Thank you for joining me on this journey of self-discovery and growth. It is my sincere hope that "Value Your Time" has enriched your life and inspired you to embrace the value of time.

Remember that the journey of valuing your time is ongoing.

Embrace each moment with intention and purpose. Embrace each challenge as an opportunity for growth. Embrace each day as a gift and use it wisely.

As you embark on your continued journey, I wish you success, fulfillment, and a life filled with purpose. May you live each day to the fullest, appreciating the gift of time and using it to create a positive impact on your life and the lives of those around you.

Thank you once again for allowing me to be a part of your journey. May your path be filled with joy, meaning, and the realization of your deepest aspirations.

With warmest regards,

CREGG HAMPTON

Afterword

As we come to the end of "Value Your Time," I want to extend my heartfelt gratitude to each and every one of you who have embarked on this transformative journey with me. It has been an honor and a privilege to share the principles of time management and personal growth with you, and I hope that this book has left a lasting impact on your life.

The journey of valuing our time is a lifelong pursuit—a continuous effort to optimize our time and make the most of every moment. It is not a destination but a path that leads us towards greater self-awareness, intentionality, and fulfillment. As you close the final chapter of this book, I urge you to carry the essence of "Value Your Time" with you in your daily life.

Embrace the Present Moment: Life unfolds in the present moment, and our ability to embrace it with mindfulness and awareness has the power to transform our lives. Embrace each moment with a sense of gratitude and presence, knowing that the present is the only moment we truly have.

Set Clear Priorities: Understand what truly matters to you and set clear priorities aligned with your values and aspirations. Be intentional about how you allocate your time, ensuring that you invest it in activities that bring you joy, growth, and fulfillment.

Overcome Procrastination: Recognize the patterns of procrastination and take proactive steps to overcome them. Break tasks into manageable steps, set deadlines, and cultivate a sense of discipline to keep moving forward towards your goals.

Avoid Time Wasters: Be mindful of activities and habits that drain your time and energy without adding value to your life. Learn to say no to distractions and non-essential commitments, creating space for what truly matters.

Embrace Flexibility and Adaptability: Embrace change with an open mind and a willingness to adapt to new circumstances. Cultivate the ability to adjust your plans and strategies as needed, knowing that flexibility is essential in navigating life's twists and turns.

Value Work-Life Balance: Seek harmony between your personal and professional life, recognizing the importance of both in nurturing your overall well-being. Strive to find a balance that allows you to thrive in all aspects of your life.

Cultivate Healthy Habits: Harness the power of habits to create a solid foundation for your daily routines. Develop positive habits that support your goals and well-being, gradually replacing less beneficial habits with ones that serve you better.

Manage Distractions: Develop strategies to manage distractions effectively, whether they come from technology, social media, or other sources. Create a conducive environment for focus and productivity, allowing you to make the most of your time.

Embrace Continuous Improvement: Embrace a growth mindset and seek opportunities for continuous improvement in all areas of your life. Stay curious, explore new avenues, and invest in your personal and professional development.

Teach Others: As you embrace the principles of time management and personal growth, share this knowledge with others. Empower those around you to value their time and live more fulfilling lives, creating a ripple effect of positive change.

Remember that the path of valuing your time is not without challenges. There may be moments of doubt, setbacks, and obstacles along the way. Embrace these moments as opportunities for growth and learning. Each challenge you overcome will strengthen your resilience and bring you closer to the life you envision.

I encourage you to be patient with yourself as you implement the principles of "Value Your Time." The journey towards effective time management is not about achieving perfection but about progress and growth. Celebrate every step you take towards optimizing your time and making positive changes in your life.

As we part ways, I want you to know that the insights, strategies, and wisdom presented in "Value Your Time" are timeless and ever-relevant. Whether you revisit this book in the future or share its principles with others, may it continue to inspire and guide you on your journey towards a life of purpose, joy, and fulfillment.

I extend my deepest gratitude to each reader, knowing that you are the driving force behind this book's impact. Your commitment to valuing your time and embracing personal growth is a testament to the transformative power of intentional living.

If you wish to connect further, I encourage you to visit my website and explore the resources available to support your journey. I am always eager to hear from readers and learn about your experiences with "Value Your Time."

In closing, I wish you all the best on your journey of embracing the value of time. May you continue to live each day with purpose, passion, and intention, making the most of every moment and creating a life that truly reflects your values and aspirations.

Thank you for joining me on this transformative journey, and may your path be filled with joy, meaning, and the realization of your deepest dreams.

With warmest regards,

CREGG HAMPTON

Acknowledgement

Writing "Value Your Time" has been a transformative journey, and I am deeply grateful for the countless individuals who have contributed their support, guidance, and encouragement throughout this process. This book would not have been possible without the collaboration and generosity of those who have touched my life in various ways.

First and foremost, I want to express my heartfelt gratitude to my family for their unwavering love and support. To my parents, thank you for instilling in me a love for learning and a strong work ethic. Your belief in me has been a driving force behind my pursuit of knowledge and personal growth. To my siblings, thank you for always cheering me on and being my biggest fans.

I am profoundly grateful to my partner, who has been a pillar of strength and inspiration throughout this journey. Your unwavering support, encouragement, and belief in my abilities have been instrumental in bringing "Value Your Time" to life.

I extend my sincere appreciation to my team at Time Mastery Academy for their dedication and hard work. Your commitment to our shared vision has been instrumental in empowering individuals and organizations to optimize their time and achieve their goals.

I am grateful to my mentors and advisors who have provided invaluable guidance and insights throughout this writing process. Your wisdom and expertise have enriched this book and shaped my understanding of time management and personal development.

I would like to extend my thanks to my editor for their meticulous attention to detail and constructive feedback, which have helped shape "Value Your Time" into its final form.

My gratitude also extends to the research community for their contributions to the field of time management. The works of numerous researchers, authors, and thought leaders have laid the foundation for the principles presented in this book.

I am thankful for the opportunity to collaborate with fellow authors and professionals who have enriched my understanding of time management and personal growth. Your shared insights and experiences have broadened my perspective and enriched the content of "Value Your Time."

To the readers and audiences who have attended my workshops and presentations, thank you for your enthusiasm and willingness to embrace the principles of time management. Your questions, feedback, and stories have been a constant source of inspiration.

I would also like to express my appreciation to my agent and publisher for their belief in the value of "Value Your Time" and for helping to bring this book to a global audience.

Lastly, I want to acknowledge the collective effort of all the individuals working behind the scenes—the designers, illustrators, marketers, and everyone else who contributed to making this book a reality.

To each and every person who has supported me on this journey, whether through words of encouragement, constructive criticism, or a simple act of kindness, I extend my deepest gratitude. Your belief in the importance of valuing time and embracing personal growth has been a driving force behind "Value Your Time."

Writing this book has been an immensely rewarding experience, and I am grateful to have the opportunity to share these insights with the world. My hope is that "Value Your Time" serves as a guiding light, empowering readers to embrace the value of time and live more fulfilling lives.

Thank you for being a part of this journey. May we continue to learn, grow, and make the most of every moment, embracing each day with intention, purpose, and joy.

With profound gratitude,

CREGG HAMPTON

READING REFERENCES

"Value Your Time" is a comprehensive exploration of time management and personal growth, and I encourage readers to further expand their understanding by delving into additional resources on these topics. Below are some recommended references that complement the principles presented in this book:

"**The 7 Habits of Highly Effective People**" by Stephen R. Covey - In this classic self-help book, Covey outlines seven powerful habits that can transform the way we approach life and work. The principles of proactivity, prioritization, and time management align closely with the concepts explored in "Value Your Time."

"**Atomic Habits: An Easy & Proven Way to Build Good Habits & Break Bad Ones**" by James Clear - Clear's book delves into the science of habit formation, offering practical strategies to create positive habits that can enhance productivity and well-being.

"**Deep Work: Rules for Focused Success in a Distracted World**" by Cal Newport - In this thought-provoking book, Newport explores the value of deep, concentrated work and provides strategies to minimize distractions and optimize productivity.

"**Essentialism: The Disciplined Pursuit of Less**" by Greg McKeown - McKeown advocates for a focused and deliberate approach to decision-making, emphasizing the importance of saying no to non-essential activities and prioritizing what truly matters.

"**Mindfulness in Plain English**" by Bhante Henepola Gunaratana - For those interested in delving deeper into mindfulness, this book offers practical guidance on the practice of meditation and mindfulness in everyday life.

"**Eat That Frog!: 21 Great Ways to Stop Procrastinating and Get More Done in Less Time**" by Brian Tracy - Tracy presents a collection of practical time management techniques and strategies to overcome procrastination and improve productivity.

"**The Power of Now: A Guide to Spiritual Enlightenment**" by Eckhart Tolle - Tolle's book explores the concept of living in the present moment and embracing mindfulness as a means to find inner peace and purpose.

"**Digital Minimalism: Choosing a Focused Life in a Noisy World**" by Cal Newport - In this book, Newport delves into the impact of technology on our lives and provides insights on how to use digital tools mindfully to enhance productivity and well-being.

"**Thrive: The Third Metric to Redefining Success and Creating a Life of Well-Being, Wisdom, and Wonder**" by Arianna Huffington - Huffington advocates for a more holistic approach to success, one that encompasses well-being, wisdom, and a sense of wonder in addition to professional achievements.

"**The Miracle Morning: The Not-So-Obvious Secret Guaranteed to Transform Your Life (Before 8 AM)**" by Hal Elrod - Elrod presents a morning routine that incorporates mindfulness, personal development, and goal-setting to start the day with intention and energy.

"**Getting Things Done: The Art of Stress-Free Productivity**" by David Allen - Allen's book offers a system for organizing tasks and managing commitments to reduce stress and increase productivity.

"The One Thing: The Surprisingly Simple Truth Behind Extraordinary Results" by Gary Keller and Jay Papasan - This book emphasizes the importance of focusing on one critical task at a time and eliminating distractions to achieve extraordinary results.

"The Power of Habit: Why We Do What We Do in Life and Business" by Charles Duhigg - Duhigg explores the science of habit formation and how understanding and changing our habits can lead to significant personal growth.

"Essential Time Management Techniques: Stop Procrastination, Improve Productivity, and Achieve Success" by John Adair - This practical guide to time management offers a variety of techniques and strategies to optimize time and achieve personal and professional goals.

"Flow: The Psychology of Optimal Experience" by Mihaly Csikszentmihalyi - Csikszentmihalyi examines the concept of "flow," a state of heightened focus and enjoyment in tasks, and how it can lead to increased productivity and life satisfaction.

These references cover a wide range of topics related to time management, personal growth, mindfulness, and productivity. I encourage readers to explore the ones that resonate most with their interests and goals. The pursuit of personal development and time mastery is an ongoing journey, and the insights gained from these resources can complement and enhance the principles presented in "Value Your Time."

∞∞∞